PRAISE FOR *THE PIT*

"*The Pit* is a brilliant tribute to those individuals who stand between us and death — the physicians who staff our nation's emergency rooms. In exquisite, sensitive detail, ER physician Gary Conrad describes how both joy and pathos are everyday experiences for this dedicated group of medical professionals. One moment an ER doc may remove a bug from the ear of a screaming four-year old, the next moment s/he may perform CPR on an adult who may not survive. *The Pit* is likely to become a classic in the autobiographical medical literature. As I read this gripping account, I found myself thinking: If I'm ever ambulanced to the ER, I hope Dr. Gary Conrad is on duty."

Larry Dossey, M.D., author of *One Mind: How Our Individual Mind Is Part of a Greater Consciousness and Why It Matters*

"Tragedy, humor, frenzy, exhaustion, medical riddles, occasional triumph — the emergency department has everything. Dr. Conrad has seen it all, and he takes us on an often poignant tour with the confidence, grace, and wry wit of a true veteran. A thoroughly engaging, satisfying read."

David Abercrombie, M.D.

"An insightful look at the intense, stressful, sometimes horrifying world of the emergency physician. You will not come away from this book unaffected. This may be Conrad's best work yet."

William Bernhardt, author of *The Last Chance Lawyer*

"One does need a modicum of brain power and a willingness to work and study hard to be a decent doctor. But to be a true healer requires a different and far more important set of traits — these include empathy, generosity, kindness, and (maybe most important) a willingness to be self-critical and to laugh at one's own foibles. And these latter qualities almost jump off the pages of Gary Conrad's latest memoir."

Jerome R Hoffman, MA MD
Professor of Medicine Emeritus
UCLA School of Medicine

"As a colleague of Gary's for almost thirty years, I was aware of some of these stories, but I was amazed at how many were new to me. Yet, I had experienced profoundly similar events in my career. I would not have the honesty or intestinal fortitude to bare these experiences on paper as Gary has courageously done, though I can tell this has been a therapeutic exercise for him. What I love most about the book is his acknowledgement of the most underpaid, underappreciated instruments of God . . . nurses. Without them, there would be total chaos in the medical world. Well done, Gary! You have captured the essence of life in a medical student, resident, and emergency physician. Gary is living proof that a proper mix of honesty, humility and spirituality will get you by, even in the most difficult of circumstances."

Dan D. Donnell, M.D.

"When Gary Conrad arrived in our emergency department in July of 1978, I worked alongside him for many years. His descriptive stories from *The Pit* demonstrate the empathy and skill that he and the nursing staff shared in providing urgent care 24/7. As you will read, Gary's spiritual belief system assisted him greatly in providing that care. Those who labor in the emergency department are a special breed who thrive in the midst of chaos, prepared for any event at any time. I treasure my relationship with Gary, his fellow physicians and nursing staff who provided high quality emergency care over the years. Those times were some of the best of my life, and I'll never forget them."

Ann Warzyn, RN, BSN,
former Nurse Director

"I have been anxiously awaiting the completion of *The Pit*, and it did not disappoint! The book provides a glimpse of the experiences of Dr. Gary Conrad from medical school to practicing as an emergency physician. I was blessed to work with him in the emergency department as a RN for around seventeen years and still consider him a friend, even after the snake prank (you need to read the book) that I now laugh about. Some of the recollections will bring laughter and others are deadly serious and painful to read. The stories recounted by Dr. Conrad triggered not only many of my own memories from the emergency department, but also reminded me of the closeness and trust shared by the team of people who work there."

Pam Tucker, MSN, RN

"Dr Gary Conrad takes us on another adventure, but this time through his memories of survival and triumph in *The Pit*. As a Family Medicine doctor and fellow alumnus of the University of Arizona Integrative Medicine Fellowship, I shared many of Dr Conrad's memories of medical school as well as residency and early medical practice. As has become his style, he delivers difficult subjects with a keen insight into the human psyche and sprinkles in humor and hilarious sayings that caught me off guard and made me chuckle. This is a must read for medical professionals or anyone interested in the inner workings of The Pit from the point of view of a seasoned ER doc."

Robert Edwards, M.D.

"I have had the privilege of knowing Gary for over 35 years including working as a paramedic for a dozen years, both bringing him critical patients and witnessing his clinical acumen on many, many occasions. I found the writing to be captivating and elicited many raw, unexpected emotions. His compelling recollections of his training and practice as an emergency physician demonstrated the sometimes overwhelming demands and challenges faced in emergency medicine."

Keith Tucker

"Gary D. Conrad has captured the essence of a life dedicated to working in the emergency department. Conrad's assiduous storytelling hits all the right marks and takes the reader into the mind of the true 'pit' doctor."

Michael Padgham, M.D.

THE
PIT

Memoir of an
EMERGENCY Physician

GARY D. CONRAD, M.D.

THE PIT: Memoir of an **EMERGENCY** Physician
Copyright © 2019 by Gary D. Conrad
Softcover ISBN: 978-1-7335591-1-9

Ahimsa Press

Published by Ahimsa Press
3126 S. Boulevard St., #285
Edmond, OK 73013
Website: GaryDConrad.com

Cover photo by Fariha Rafa
Cover design by Steve Boaldin
Interior design by Marilyn Ratzlaff

Written, Printed and Produced in the United States of America

CONTENTS

To Dr. Andrew Weil

My mentor, colleague and friend

Because of your life, the world is a better place

BEGINNINGS

March 19, 2014

I woke at 3:45 a.m. and lay in bed, restless, my wife sleeping quietly by my side. I struggled to return to dreamland, knowing I had to rise early that morning to work a ten-hour shift in the emergency department at my hospital. While the general public knows it as the emergency room or "ER," those in the field of emergency medicine know that 'emergency room' is an outdated phrase, going back to the time when emergency treatment areas were small affairs, perhaps one or two patient rooms. Nowadays, depending upon the size of the hospital, the emergency department is usually a multi-room complex, staffed by many different health care providers. Also, for reasons which you are soon to discover, those who labor there sardonically call the emergency department, "The Pit." But I digress . . .

That particular morning, I tried to relax and still myself, even though my mind was on overdrive, thinking back to four days earlier, when I'd decided to author a collection of stories based on my many varied experiences in medical school, internship and eventually as an emergency medicine physician. On that day, I had created an outline of the intended chapters and began to write.

Why now, after all these years? I wondered as I lay there. So far in my writing career, I had created two books, was laboring on a third, and in these works my publisher had asked if I wanted to put "M.D." following my name. Believing being a doctor had little to do with composing novels, I resisted. Now, though, I felt it was time to embrace the part of me that was an emergency physician and proudly write about my experiences as "Gary D. Conrad, M.D."

But, on that early morning, it occurred to me that by deciding to write this book, I had inadvertently unlocked and opened my own personal Pandora's box, and I was relentlessly assaulted by its contents—buried memories that I had long ago either repressed or simply put aside. In my mind, I relived recollections of incredibly funny moments, times of camaraderie, of living, of dying, of deeply joyful and painful events. Some even made me gasp as I recalled them, though they happened so many years ago.

Lying in bed, I tried to stuff the cascade of memories back into the box, but much like Pandora of lore, once unleashed, they could not be returned. So, I gave in and let them flow and move through my mind, looking at them much as I would watch surging water while sitting in front of a rolling river. With time and love directed at them, I was convinced the powerful energies associated with certain memories would dissipate and lose their grip on me, but at their own pace, on their own schedule. For the present moment, I just had to feel them. I had no escape.

Over the weeks following this pre-dawn moment of crisis, I began to feel an aura of excitement about the creation of this work. Knowing there were many tales I had likely forgotten, to help jog my memory I decided to enlist the help of some of the emergency nurses who had worked with me through the years, and overall, they were most excited about helping me with this grand project. A meeting with the nurses was arranged and I, along with another physician colleague, sat with them as they recounted one amazing story after another.

Two narrations, in particular, profoundly moved me. One nurse related that many years ago she had cared for a man who was experiencing a sickle cell crisis, an event that occurs in those with sickle cell anemia. In this medical emergency, sickle-shaped red blood cells clump like a log jam and block the flow of blood and oxygen to the tissues, causing excruciating pain. The patient's discomfort was severe and intractable in spite of treatment with oxygen, IV fluids and high doses of pain medicine. Over and over again the patient asked, "Am I going to be okay?" Repeatedly, she told him, "You're going to be fine." In spite of doing all that she and the physician could for the patient, he died some hours later. The guilt the nurse experienced was overwhelming, and she wondered: *Should I have been honest with him and shared that he was in critical condition? Could I have done something different, some intervention—anything— that might have saved his life?*

Another shared that, as a very young nurse, she had cared for a man whose legs had been mangled as he had sat on the back of a sanitation truck when it was rear-ended by another vehicle. One of his legs was completely severed, and the other leg was attached only by a thin layer of skin. His legs were horribly crushed, so much so that reattachment was not an option. The attending physician asked the nurse to cut the remaining tissue so the still-attached leg could be removed. But, after doing so, in her youthful mind, she felt responsible for the loss of the man's leg. Although the nurse was simply performing her job, she was greatly traumatized by the event.

With stories like these in mind, I recalled when I went to a medical conference some years ago. One of the speakers asked the audience, "I want you to write down some words you might say to a patient with whom you have unfinished business."

Note pads were distributed, and during the next twenty minutes or so, the room was shrouded in complete silence as the group feverishly wrote their tales. I should have known something was up when, towards the end of the writing session, boxes of tissue paper were distributed to the audience.

Once the compositions were completed, the speaker asked us to individually read to the group what we had written. Professional after professional began to relate terribly painful events, times they missed diagnoses, moments more words of comfort or explanation should have been offered, times when things went horribly wrong.

Before long, not only were the readers sobbing uncontrollably, so were many of those listening. No doubt, these recollections brought back some of the listeners' own painful memories and the guilt and shame associated with them. What these tales had in common with mine is that very long ago these incidents created invisible wounds, which, to this day, are still deeply troubling.

Other nurses in my emergency department, ones who had not recounted their stories in our meeting, suffered equally traumatizing experiences. On more than one occasion over the years, after dealing with an especially difficult case, I would discover a nurse crying alone in the break room. The pain was just too intense. As hard as it is to believe in this day and age, counseling for such ordeals was simply not available in times past.

Years ago, as a young physician, when I began laboring in the emergency department, I thought I was uniquely suited to handle the taxing job of being an emergency physician. I ate a pescatarian diet, exercised regularly, followed a fulfilling meditation practice, and most important of all, had a very short memory about the difficult events of the day.

But none of us in medicine is Superman or Superwoman, and no matter how strong we view ourselves to be, the fact is that each of us has pockets of painful memories tucked inside, neatly stowed away and sequestered deep within our consciousness. For us to be as mentally healthy as possible, the many seals which secure these recollections have to be snapped open and the contents within aired out and explored. It's a task, whether in medicine or not, we all should perform at some point in time in our journey through this earthly existence. Now, though, it's my turn, and I embrace the sharing with great joy and more than a little trepidation. My kaleidoscope of medical tales awaits you.

Oh, by the way, if you happen to hear soft weeping from somewhere in the distant background, don't be alarmed.

It's just me—healing.

Chapter 1

A GOOD MAN

An emergency department is a stress pit, a lake of exhaustion washing over all who work there. The demanding environment smothers physicians, nurses, paramedics, EMTs, and anyone else who dares enter the battle zone in the war to save lives. For over thirty-eight years, I have worked as an emergency physician. I know the terms of engagement.

For physicians, in particular, one of our most difficult duties comes with informing family members that their loved one has died. How I wish the Grim Reaper, with his frightening black robe and scythe, was a less familiar figure in emergency medicine, but he's not. He's always lurking in some dark, secluded corner, hoping to collect his prey, and to his endless delight, the targets continue to arrive. Hardly a week goes by that I don't see a patient who presents in cardiac arrest and dies, despite our efforts.

Some families, recognizing the deteriorating condition of their loved ones, prepare for death by having DNR (Do Not Resuscitate) papers signed, and perhaps have arranged Hospice care. With these measures in place, the terminally ill one is given the chance to die peacefully at home.

But sometimes there are those, in seemingly good health, whose heart unexpectedly stops, and they come to me strapped to a stretcher in the back of a speeding, careening ambulance with lights flashing and sirens blaring. Soon afterward, terrified family members show up at the emergency department, clinging to the hope that somehow, someway, their loved one was pulled from the bank of the River Styx, back into the land of the living.

I understand why families cling to such belief. Nearly every medical show on television has amazingly high resuscitation rates, creating the expectation that health and recovery wait in the emergency department. The assumption leaves the physician with a difficult problem in explaining an emergency death to a family who do not realize that, in the real world, in spite of our technological advances, the overall chance of survival after cardiac arrest is abysmally low.

In reflection, I admit that, as medical students, we were never given a course on how to tell family members about the death of their beloved one. Rather, by observing our attending and resident physicians, we formulated our own way of handling this most challenging task. Perhaps, in this day and age, with medical humanism coming more and more to the forefront, this important skill is taught.

As an emergency physician, when someone dies, I do the very best I can to inform families of their loved one's death in a caring and professional manner. That said, in spite of my years of experience in performing this demanding task, it has not become easier, and I don't expect it to.

When a patient has passed away, usually, the process goes something like this. Shortly after I have pronounced the patient dead, I enter the family room with the deceased's chart in hand and introduce myself. After sitting down and facing the family, I don't delay in telling the bad news. People don't want to hear a long, drawn-out story before I announce the dreaded truth. As quickly and gently as possible, I let them know their loved one has died. After they've had some moments to grieve, I ask to hear the story of the events surrounding the death so I can tell their family doctor, and later the medical examiner, the details of what happened. Empathy and expression of my sorrow for their loss are important to provide, for at this critical moment they are likely as vulnerable as they have ever been; the world they live in has been changed forever.

Most of the time, the members of the family are too stunned to have much to say, but on one particular occasion, I remember a very different ending to the conversation, one that will be forever imprinted in my mind.

One chilly winter day, I was scurrying around the emergency department, trying to keep up with crowds of sick people, when one of the nurses approached me, scratching some notes on a yellow pad.

"Doctor Conrad, the ambulance is bringing in a seventy-eight year old male in cardiac arrest. Their ETA is ten minutes."

"Was it witnessed?" I asked, knowing that those who are by themselves when their heart stops—and don't receive immediate CPR—are very unlikely to be resuscitated.

"No. He was last seen two hours before."

"What was his initial rhythm?"

"Asystole."

No heartbeat at all. *Not good*, I thought.

"What is it now?"

"Still asystole."

"How long have they been working the patient?"

"Thirty minutes."

I shook my head, thinking: *This patient doesn't have a prayer, but we'll do what we can.*

Promptly ten minutes later, I was waiting in the Code Room

with several emergency nurses, when I heard the sound of an opening door and smelled the exhaust of an ambulance. In seconds, the paramedic and EMT hurriedly rolled the patient into the room, IVs hanging from both arms. A fireman was performing chest compressions, while another was giving oxygen by ventilating him through an endotracheal tube, a hollow plastic tube the paramedic had placed in the patient's airway.

They moved the patient from their stretcher to ours, where I performed a quick examination while CPR was in progress. The patient looked older than seventy-eight. *Must have been sick for a while,* I thought. My initial inspection revealed his pupils were fixed and dilated. No cardiac sounds. No voluntary respirations. Good breath sounds with bagging. Abdomen mildly distended.

I asked the paramedic, "Update me."

Her shirt was soaked in sweat as she quickly and concisely spoke. "Mr. Evans has a long history of hypertension, non-insulin dependent diabetes mellitus and had a coronary artery bypass graft some years ago. He's on multiple cardiac meds. You've heard the report I gave to the nurse?"

"Yes."

She added, "He's still in asystole."

"How long has he been down?" I asked.

"About fifty minutes have passed since the call. Who knows how long he's actually been in arrest, though. We've been working him for around forty minutes."

"Meds?"

"Seven rounds of epinephrine, two amps of bicarb."

"When was his last does of epi?"

"Three minutes ago."

By then, the nurses had transferred the emergency department cardiac monitor to the patient.

"Stop compressions," I said to the fireman.

When he paused, I felt for a pulse and looked carefully at the rhythm on the monitor. No pulse.

Flatline.

I directed, "Confirm asystole in two leads and check for a pulse with a Doppler."

The results were as I expected; asystole was verified on the monitor, and no pulse was heard with the sensitive Doppler probe.

He's dead, I thought. *I wish there was something more I could do for him, but there's not.*

I grimly told those in attendance, "This patient is DOA. Time pronounced is 1330. Let me know when the family arrives. Good job, everyone."

Minutes later, as I worked on his chart, one of the nurses walked up and said, "The wife of the patient in the Code Room is here. She's in the family room."

"Anyone with her?" I asked.

"No."

I felt sad that the wife had to deal with the death of her husband by herself, yet I grabbed the chart and fought my way down the cold, institutional hall through a thick barrier of questions, screams and unpleasant odors. I knocked on the door of the family room, entered and discovered a slender, gray-haired, diminutive woman who appeared to be in her mid-seventies.

"I'm Doctor Gary Conrad," I said. "Are you Mrs. Evans?"
She nodded.

I pulled up a chair and sat in front of her. "I have some bad news for you. Your husband has passed away. He's dead."

Her eyes filled with tears. "I knew he was gone," she said softly.

I took a deep breath and asked, "What happened?"

"Charlie had not been in the best of health," she explained. "He went to the bedroom to take a nap this morning because he wasn't feeling well. When I went to check on him, he didn't respond

and wasn't breathing." She repressed a soft sob and put her hand to
her mouth. She took a few moments to regain her composure before
she continued, "I then called 911 and did CPR, but I felt sure I had
lost him."

"I'm so sorry," I said. "I've already talked to the paramedic,
and with Mr. Evan's past medical history, I'm certain his death will
be confirmed as natural by the medical examiner. Once that's done,
we'll take out all the tubes and you can see your husband. Do you
have any other family coming in?"

"Yes, I do, but I want to see him as soon as possible. I don't
care if the tubes are removed."

"I understand. Once we've finished speaking, his nurse will
come for you and lead you back to his room." I stood to leave and
asked, "Is there anything else I can do for you?"

"Yes, Doctor Conrad, let me tell you about my husband."

Surprised, I sat back down.

She smiled through the tears. "Many years ago, when I was
a young woman, my first husband died and left me with three small
children. Then I met Charlie Evans, my second husband-to-be, and
we fell in love. And you know what he did?"

"No."

Tears now streamed freely down her cheeks and her voice
began to break. "After we were married, he adopted my children . .
. and raised them as his own. He was a wonderful father . . . and a
good man. I will miss him terribly."

I felt my face begin to flush, and my eyes welled with tears.

She looked at me with probing brown eyes and whispered, "I
thought you should know that."

"I'm glad you told me . . . thank you." I stood and gently
squeezed her shoulder. "His nurse will be with you shortly."

I left the room and walked back to my desk, grabbing some
tissue to wipe away the tears. As I thought about what just happened, I realized that in emergency medicine we have a tendency to

dehumanize our patients, for if we know them as fathers, mothers, grandfathers, grandmothers or *any* role in life where they loved and loved deeply, it's just too painful.

Mr. Evans was more than just a body—one we tried to revive that day.

He was a good man.

Chapter 2

DOCTOR MOOSE

T he medical students I studied with, in general, were a fearless lot, seemingly immune to self-doubt. No matter what
dire straits we found ourselves entangled in, we were innova-
tive and creative enough to wiggle our way from the dark to the light,
from a crisis to a solution, wresting victory from the jaws of defeat.

Code Blue? No problem. We were aware of the drugs and
protocol to deal with cardiac arrest, and we knew the routine to follow. If patients had any chance to live, they would. *Doctor STAT?*
(Cousin to the Code Blue. While the patient is seriously ill, he or
she is not yet in cardiac arrest) No matter the situation, be it shock,
massive bleeding, stroke, heart attack, whatever, we could handle it.

The one exception to the rule of fearlessness was managing
the dreaded surgery rotation, where all bets were off. Probably the
worst part of this life-altering tour through Hell was dealing with
the surgery attendings. Even for the casual visitor to the teaching
hospital situation, the surgery attendings, also known as the head
honchos or big kahunas, weren't too hard to spot. Invariably, these

magnificent specimens of humanity had menacing scowls on their faces, as smiles were never part of their repertoire. If the corners of their mouths quivered ever so slightly, observers immediately knew that, deep inside the core of the surgery attendings, they were laughing so hard they almost fell on the floor.

If they were male, the cologne was always of the highest quality, and their hair was always neatly trimmed and combed. For a female attending, a relative rarity in the olden days, perfume or long hair was not an option. After all, in a male-dominated profession, the goal of the female attending was not to express her femininity, but rather, to blend in and not stand out from the crowd.

Whether male or female, the attending's starched white coat was the maximum length, hanging only inches from the floor, like a cloak befitting a king or queen. Their names were invariably stitched in red script just above their left upper coat pocket, which always held at least two Montblanc ink pens neatly tucked inside. Two were necessary, just in case one ran out of ink. Surgery attendings were in many ways like seasoned trekkers, ready to deal with any and all eventualities, whether that be surviving tornadic winds and rain, Everest-like snows, or stifling desert heat, fending off a marauding bear, or squatting in the wilderness and abruptly realizing that they left their roll of toilet paper back at home.

Another way to recognize the surgery attendings was by their posture. They never walked with a slump and never slouched; rather, they proudly stood as stiff as a board, chins elevated ever so slightly, as clear proof of how much better they were than everyone else.

For them, cleanliness was indeed next to godliness. Rarely would the surgery attendings walk by a sink without washing their hands or pass by a tube of sterilizing hand foam without pumping some onto the palms and briskly rubbing it in. What better way to demonstrate to the general public that their surgical procedures were always pristine and germ-free? Of course, if a post-operative infection occurred—God forbid—it must've been caused by someone

else, perhaps a nurse or a lowly technician, who broke the code of sterility during the sacred ritual of surgery.

The surgery attendings had a number of holy rules in their surgical Bibles, which they followed to the letter. These hallowed truths, having been inscribed in a small, black book by Hippocrates in the sacred depths of the ancient Grecian temples of healing, were kept under the surgery attendings' pillows, so even at night these blessed words were never too far from their colossal brains. The inviolate list included the following:

1) To cut is to cure.

2) If whatever you're doing doesn't come easy, force it.

3) My diagnosis is always correct. Anything else revealed by surgery is a result of my thoroughness in exploration.

4) All bleeding stops eventually.

5) No one dies on my watch.

6) There's no bleeding that can't be controlled by a strong-armed surgeon with a pair of hemostats.

7) When in doubt, cut it out.

8) I've only been wrong one time, and that's when I thought I was wrong, but I really wasn't.

Many other sacred axioms are known by the dwellers in the surgery inner sanctum, so sacred, in fact, that inferiors (that is, non-surgeons such as me) have never been privileged to know them.

To make matters even worse, surgery attendings seem to have a sixth sense, which allows them to detect when a medical student is around. Students should never try to tiptoe around them, hoping not to be noticed. They will be. In many ways, the surgery attendings are like bloodhounds tracking a raccoon or an escaped criminal, and students are their prey for any and all questions. The conversation might go something like this:

"What's your name, student?"

"Gary Conrad, sir."

"Are you a third year or a fourth year student?"

"Third year, sir."

"So, you want to be a doctor some day?"

"Yes sir."

"Then tell me, how many units of blood are in the human body?"

"Eight to twelve in the average adult . . . sir."

His face turns beet red and he raises his eyebrows ever so slightly. I know he's wondering how I actually knew the answer. He clears his throat and gruffly asks, "How many ccs are in each unit?"

"Around 500 ccs, sir."

"No, it's actually 525 ccs. Mr. Conrad, you need to read more. You'll find a very good description of blood and blood products in Schwartz, so I suggest you find your copy and study for a change."

A chuckle goes up from the nursing staff and residents in attendance. I gulp, my shoulders sag ever-so-slightly, and I say "Yes, sir." I turn to leave, properly humbled, chastened in my abject ignorance.

Now, to be completely fair, a few of the surgical attendings have been known to actually smile on occasion and, it is said, can be somewhat friendly to the residents, medical students and nursing staff, but these are the rarest of the rare. Encountering an amicable surgery attending is analogous to finding a 1909 S VDB penny in your pocket change, seeing a dodo bird on the side of the road while you're driving to work, or being hit by a meteor while you are out mowing the front yard.

But the generic surgery attendings are virtual slapstick comedians when compared to the species known as the thoracic surgery attending. He or she makes all the others look like wimps, like a feral alley cat compared to a pampered house tabby. One such person where I trained was Doctor Edward Moose, affectionately called Doctor "Bull Moose" by those who thought he had some similarity in appearance to Theodore Roosevelt.

To me, Doctor Moose looked completely different from the

warm and cuddly Teddy. He was pale from too many hours in the surgical suite, had short, black hair with a matching moustache, and his angry, steely stare and icy, probing questions would make the most secure and stable medical students spontaneously wet their pants and scurry to the bathroom to take care of the impending episode of stress-induced diarrhea. He was that bad, and everyone, including his fellow surgeons, was scared of him. While I never had to face him personally, the tales of his nefarious and vindictive nature found their way into every conversation at the hospital, so, naturally, I made it a point to stay clear. I dared not face the wrath of Doctor Moose, who, much like the skilled surgeon he was, could dissect out a person's weaknesses and expose them for all to see, flayed like a dressed deer during hunting season.

Rumor had it that Doctor Moose was a master in the operating room, and many lives were saved because of his amazing expertise, but where was the humanity? Why did he feel the need to degrade those who worked with him? While intimidation can be a great motivator, is it necessary in the halls of learning? Doctor Moose certainly believed it was.

For years after I finished my medical school training, I was frightened of him, until one fateful day, a day I will always remember, the fear went away, never to return.

Going to the airport is, without fail, a pleasurable experience for me. It means one of two things; either I am going somewhere on a wonderful vacation or I am looking forward to returning home after spending some quality time away. One particular day, a number of years ago, I was in a light and happy mood as I was coming back from one such trip, when far down the corridor of the Oklahoma City's Will Rogers World Airport, I spotted a familiar face walking my way, one that had been forever etched in my memory.

Heaven help me, I thought, *it's Doctor Moose!*

My first urge was to let loose a blood-curdling scream and

run in the opposite direction, as I clearly recalled how bad, Medusa-like things happened to those who looked him in the eyes. *Where can I go where he won't see me? Maybe I could hide in the janitorial closet? The bathroom?* I shook my head to clear my mind. As I thought about it, I realized I was letting fears that had occurred over thirty years earlier influence my current behavior. Obviously, it was time to deal with the feelings I had way back when, but what to do now, in the present moment? *Do I just walk by and ignore him? No,* I thought, *that would be sweeping my fear under the rug. It was time for action, but what?*

He walked closer . . . and closer. The hackles on my neck began to rise, and I broke out into a cold sweat. I focused on my breath and tried to calm myself. Suddenly, I had an inspiration. As he walked next to me, I moved over to face him, shook his hand and calmly said, "Hi Ed." I noticed him wince ever so slightly as I called him by his first name. "I know you don't remember me, but I was a medical student in the '70s when you were a thoracic surgery attending. It's good to see you again."

He blankly nodded at me and didn't say a word.

With that I grinned, turned and walked away. When I glanced back, I noticed a stunned, confused look on his face.

I was all smiles as I continued down the airport walkway, knowing I had—at long last—overcome my fears and gone face-to-face with Doctor Moose, a man I had previously feared greatly. No longer was he like a hellish demon, with horns protruding from both sides of his head and hair made of snakes, rather, he was like, as my old football coach used to say, "—an ordinary guy who puts his pants on one leg at a time, just like you do."

Now, in retrospect, I can't help but wonder if Doctor Moose was really as bad as everyone said he was. Whether he was or wasn't doesn't really matter, for if I look at the situation with a new set of eyes, I realize that most of those who are aggressive and demeaning to others usually act from a place of personal insecurity. When others are put down, the attacker rises to a level where the maligned ones are less likely to challenge him or her.

Nevertheless, I'm thrilled beyond words that I'm no longer afraid of Doctor Moose. Perhaps if I see him again, I'll ask him to spend an evening with me for a cup of Darjeeling tea, and we can talk over old times.

Well, come to think of it, maybe not . . .

Chapter 3

EXPECT THE UNEXPECTED

Many years ago I was working in the emergency department when a paramedic called in a patient report. They were
coming in hot—lights and sirens—with a young woman in
cardiac arrest.

I was at the desk when they arrived through the ambulance
entrance, though I immediately jumped up and followed the entou-
rage into the treatment room. I glanced at the patient as they rolled
her in on a stretcher; she was ashen in color and appeared to be in
her mid-20s. A fireman was performing chest compressions on the
patient, while an EMT, an emergency medical technician, was giving
her oxygen through a tube the paramedic had placed in her trachea.

The paramedic gave me a quick report. "Twenty-seven year
old white female—"

"Twenty-seven?" I interrupted.

"Yes, twenty-seven. She had a witnessed cardiac arrest this
morning at her home. CPR was started by a family member."

"How long have you worked her?"

"Thirty minutes. She was in asystole when we arrived and was cyanotic. So, I put a tube into her airway, with good breath sounds heard afterward, but she never started breathing on her own and her color never improved. Her pupils were fixed and dilated at the scene, and they still are. She's had multiple rounds of epi and atropine, and I just pushed two amps of bicarb. She's got some blood on the back of her head where she fell."

"I see."

"So far no response," he added.

I couldn't help but wonder why such a youthful woman had an event like this—possibly a heart attack? Granted, heart disease currently is affecting more young adults because of poor diet, sedentary lifestyle and smoking, among other risk factors, but still this was most unusual; it just didn't make sense.

My instincts growled at me. Something was wrong, and I knew it. *What was it?* I wondered.

I did a brief examination, confirmed that the endotracheal tube was properly placed, and I noted a small amount of blood oozing from the back of her head. I continued the cascade of drugs for far longer than I should have, for she was young—too young—and she deserved everything I had to offer.

Thirty minutes later, I reluctantly pronounced her dead.

I asked the nurse in charge, "Any family here yet?"

"No," she responded.

Where could they be? I thought. *This didn't make sense either. Why give her CPR and not immediately come to the hospital?*

Now that the intensity of the moment had passed, I decided to take a closer look at her. I was especially curious about the source of bleeding from her head. After putting on a pair of latex gloves, I lifted her head up and palpated the wound. I expected to find a cut or laceration, but instead, as I carefully pressed against the bloodied area, I felt a small defect in her skull, one that shouldn't have occurred from a simple fall.

I called x-ray to take some films of her skull. The technician grumbled about the ridiculousness of shooting an x-ray on a dead person, but eventually he relented and came to take the films. Once the x-rays were developed, the cause of the woman's death was no longer in question.

A bullet was lodged in the middle of her brain.

Questions swirled in my mind. *Who shot her? Why? And was it the same person who supposedly witnessed her collapse and gave CPR?* But this was no TV show, and I was not Sherlock Holmes. These questions would have to be answered by the police.

In emergency medicine, the physician learns that complacency is the enemy of a good diagnosis. Nothing is ever as easy or straightforward as it seems. There always seems to be a snake lurking in the grass, a trap just waiting to lure you into a mistaken assumption. A good emergency physician knows to take a second look at everything. When a diagnosis is obvious, think again—it probably isn't. One has to be as a carpenter, who measures twice and cuts once.

In the emergency department, one should expect the unexpected.

Chapter 4

HELPLESS

My first year in a family practice residency was the year from Hell, and I had no idea what sort of chaotic nightmare I was getting into when I matched with this program while I was in my final year of medical school. In this setting, senior residents from nearby university programs came to supervise us, and not only were the hours long, sometimes up to thirty-six hours at a stretch, but also the responsibilities we had to shoulder were enormous.

The fringe benefit of this onerous load was that many procedures came my way, ones which otherwise would have been passed on to a more experienced specialty resident. For example, while there I performed an appendectomy, a Cesarean section, a vasectomy and an amputation, all operations rarely performed by first year family practice residents.

Amazing learning experiences came to me, but at the dubious cost of having no personal life whatsoever. I lost weight and could barely wear my clothes, which grew more loose-fitting and scarecrow-like as the year went on. I was like a zombie that rarely saw the light of day, one who spent his life listlessly roaming the craggy depths of the Earth, somehow forgetting what the sun looked and felt like. While I learned at an exponential rate, my exposure to extremely challenging cases increased in measure. On one such occasion, I helped care for a patient so trying, that even to this day, I shudder as I think about the experience.

A week or so before my rotation in surgery started, a young woman named Kim had been severely injured in a motor vehicle accident. When she was brought in by ambulance, she was determined to have a number of significant traumatic injuries and required major abdominal surgery, which included a splenectomy and repair of a liver laceration. In addition, a tube had to be placed in her airway to help her breathe. In the days following her surgery, she developed difficulty breathing, and she was diagnosed with a dreaded complication of severe trauma, Adult Respiratory Distress Syndrome (ARDS).

ARDS is a condition that occurs when fluid accumulates in the alveoli (air sacs) of the lungs. The collecting fluid makes the lungs heavy and stiff, restricting their ability to expand properly and decreasing the oxygen level in the blood. About a third of those who get ARDS will eventually die, and those who do recover almost always have some degree of permanent lung damage. Unfortunately, lung transplantation is not a practical option for those with ARDS, as these patients are usually critically ill, and lung transplants are generally attempted only in those who are clinically stable.

When our surgical team first began making rounds on Kim, I discovered her to be a lovely young woman in her mid-twenties. She was of medium build, and her mid-length, light brown hair was highlighted with streaks of blonde. Her abdomen was now marred by a long, vertical surgical incision, one that stretched from the upper part of her abdomen to the lower, curving around her umbilicus. She was Caucasian, somewhat pale, and unable to speak because of the breathing tube inserted in her throat. She could communicate only by gesturing with her hands or writing on a pad.

Eventually a tracheostomy — a surgical opening placed in the throat to secure the airway — was performed, and while she was still unable to talk, she could then at least mouth words that were usually understandable. In spite of our efforts, though, over the weeks her condition continued to worsen. She required more and more oxygen delivered to her through the ventilator, and the mechanical pressure required to keep the lungs open had to be raised to extremely high levels just to maintain her oxygen at a survivable level. Serial chest x-rays showed gradual, insidious worsening of her condition, but fortunately she never developed the feared complication of such elevated pressures, a collapsed lung.

Emotions run high in the hospital setting, and I still recall how attached Kim became to her assigned resident, James, a slender family practice resident with combed-back brown hair and black frame glasses with thick lenses. I felt certain by his mannerisms that he cared at least as much for her. Once during rounds, with the attending physician and residents present, she mouthed to him, "I love you." Embarrassed, he did not respond, as, in theory at least, a dictum of our practice demands that medical personnel are not to become emotionally involved with our patients.

One day a Code Blue was called to Kim's room. This alert has the well-deserved reputation as the most serious emergency in a hospital, a stoppage of a patient's heart or breathing. I, along with my fellow residents, dashed to her bedside and found her to be blue and unresponsive, with a dangerously low pulse rate. To our dismay, we realized that her ARDS had worsened, so much so that the pressure required to ventilate her lungs had finally exceeded the ability of the respirator to maintain it.

James quickly removed Kim's respirator tubing, attached a breathing bag to her tracheostomy tube and began to manually breathe for her with one hundred percent oxygen. He had barely enough strength in his hands to squeeze the air into her lungs, and soon a thin sheen of sweat began to appear on this forehead. Tears formed in the corners of his eyes.

In a matter of seconds, as her oxygen level began to improve, her pulse rate increased, and she slowly regained consciousness. Initially, she thrashed about in confusion, and as she became more alert, she looked from side to side, her eyes screaming in terror to all of us. She knew, as we all knew, she was on the verge of death. I'll never forget that look of fear and panic in her eyes—never—as long as I live. I felt my heart in my throat.

I thought: *Oh God . . . help her . . . help James . . . help me . . .*

Tears now freely flowed down James' face. The scene in the room was beyond horrible—there was nothing else we could do to assist her. No more wonders of technology, no more modern drugs— we were helpless.

Moments later, the chief surgical resident arrived in the room and moved to Kim's side. He put on his stethoscope and listened to her chest. Dropping the stethoscope back into his coat pocket, he shook his head and quietly said, "Her breath sounds are equal, and her trachea is not deviated to either side. There is no pneumothorax."

He paused for a moment, and then grimly whispered to James, "There's nothing more we can do. Stop . . . it's time to stop."

At these words, James glanced down at Kim, who also heard what was said by the surgical resident. Her panic-stricken eyes begged James to continue. Using all the force he could muster, James gave her a few more breaths, and then averted his eyes to escape her stare. He sighed deeply and reluctantly unhooked the breathing bag. We all stood by and watched her writhe as she suffocated. She eventually became blue and comatose, and within a short time, it was over.

Even in death, Kim was still beautiful.

Goddammit.

Chapter 5

THE FETUS

E very senior at the University of Oklahoma Medical School
was required to do a rotation in a small town in rural Oklahoma. While this experience was allegedly for learning, I'm
certain that the underlying reason was the hope that at least some
of the medical students would be attracted to practice in the under-
served rural settings, where physicians were, and continue to be, desperately needed.

Whatever the purpose, at that stage in our medical careers,
we had finished all of our basic rotations and had some semblance
of clinical skills. We were ready—at least we thought we were—for
such a challenge. Since my grandparents, Harold and Ruth Conrad,
lived in southwest Oklahoma, I chose to do my rotation at a nearby
community hospital.

For most students, going to the small communities was quite
a culture shock. Up to this time in our training, we'd had the benefit
of being surrounded by many well-trained specialists. But, out in the
sticks, as we in the city jokingly called the countryside, the severity of

the illnesses of patients to be dealt with was at least as high as in the more populated areas, but help from certain specialists simply wasn't available. As the old saying goes, we had to "fly by the seat of our pants" at times and handle these tough cases as best we could. If the problems of the patients were too complex for us to manage, we did all we could to stabilize them before arranging transfer to the nearest medical Mecca. As I experienced this type of practice personally, I developed a whole new respect for the physicians who labored in small towns, who were truly dedicated and fearless as they provided quality medical care. They were, no doubt, a breed apart.

While on this small town rotation, I lived in a sleep room at the hospital, ate my meals in the cafeteria, and except for occasional visits to my grandparents, I was available 24/7 for anyone who needed my help. Most of the time, I was ensconced in the emergency department taking care of generally minor health issues, but one night, in the wee hours of the morning, I was urgently summoned for a hospital emergency, of a kind I hope I never have to confront again.

The day had been long and hard and I was exhausted. Around two a.m., when the emergency department became as quiet as an owl-less cemetery at midnight, I walked to my sleep room and bedded down, hoping to get some shuteye. Ten minutes later, I was dead asleep and dreaming when the bedside phone rang.

"Is this Gary Conrad, the medical student?" a frantic voice asked.

"Yes," I somehow managed to mutter in my stupor.

"I'm Sue, an RN up in labor and delivery. We need you to come here STAT."

"What's up?"

"Just come. You're needed now." There was a click, and the line went dead.

Ill-humored, fatigued and still half asleep, I hurriedly popped out of my cozy, warm bed, threw on my glasses and stumbled out of the door and into the cold hospital air. I rubbed the goosebumps covering my arms as I dashed down the hallway. I took the elevator up to the second floor, and in moments I rushed through the doors of the labor and delivery suite. A moaning woman was up in stirrups on the delivery table, and the pungent smell of Betadine filled the air. A stout young woman in nursing garb greeted me.

"You Gary Conrad?"

"Yes."

"I'm Sue, the nurse. I'll make it quick. This young woman, Mrs. Hayward, is nineteen years old and this is her first pregnancy. She presented in labor just moments ago. She has received no prenatal care, but she's in active labor and pushing. The family doctor on call is on his way, but we need you here in case she delivers before he arrives."

"How many weeks into her pregnancy is she?"

"That's the problem, and the main reason I called you. By dates she is somewhere around twenty weeks gestation."

"Only twenty?" I questioned, knowing that the accepted minimum age of fetal viability is considered to be around twenty-four weeks.

"Yes," the nurse confirmed. "Let's hope that she's farther along than we think, but her abdomen is too small for her to be full term."

"I see. How dilated is she?"

"She is complete—fully dilated."

"Fetal heart tones?"

She replied, "Normal at one hundred-forty."

With those words, a scream came up from the table.

The nurse glared at me and pointed to a nearby table with supplies on the top. She ordered, "Get ready!"

I quickly donned a surgical hat, sterile gown and gloves. I sat on a stool at the foot of the patient's bed.

"Mrs. Hayward?" I questioned.

"Yes?"

"I need to check you. Are you still having a contraction?"

"No, it stopped."

"Then can you let your legs open a little more?"

"Yes, but I need something for the pain."

"I'm sorry, but you're too far along in your labor for medication right now. It would affect the baby's breathing."

I carefully inserted my gloved index and middle fingers into her vagina until I reached the cervix, which was completely dilated, just as the nurse had said. A very small fetal head was bulging through it.

"It's time to have a baby," I said, concerned about the prematurity. "Nurse, please pull the infant warmer next to me."

To the patient, I requested, "With the next contraction, go ahead and push." I moved my hand next to the baby's head, so that I could control the delivery.

Thirty seconds passed, and with a groan, her uterus contracted and she bore down. With the pressure, the baby was forced out from the uterus into my waiting hands.

Oh no, I thought as I briefly glanced at it, *this baby is too small. It cannot survive.*

I suctioned the mucous from the baby's throat with a bulb syringe, grabbed the cord clamps, and after two were placed about an inch apart, I cut the cord between them with scissors.

With the nurse at my side, I lifted the baby up and set it on the infant warmer, where I dried it with a towel and took a closer look. Even to my untrained eye, I was certain this infant weighed far less than a pound, and the statistics were clear that survival at such a low weight was extremely rare. I noted that its eyelids were fused, which meant it could not be older than eighteen weeks. I never looked at the genitalia, because whether it was a boy or girl didn't matter. This baby was pre-viable; it could not survive. Yet, the baby did not seem to know that it wasn't supposed to live. Its will to survive was strong, and it actively moved and writhed, trying desperately to breathe, even though its lungs were not mature enough to do so.

I watched it in stunned silence, frozen by this macabre, surreal moment. In medicine, we are trained to intervene—to do something—and I ached to act, but there was nothing I could do.

I heard from somewhere in the distance, "How's my baby doing?"

"Not well," I tersely answered.

One minute—maybe two—passed, and finally the baby's movements slowed. After another minute, it stopped moving and began to turn blue. I listened to the baby's chest—no heartbeat.

I walked from the infant warmer to the head of the bed and said, "Mrs. Hayward, I'm sorry to tell you that your baby didn't make it. It was just too small to survive."

She began crying.

With that, I nodded to the nurse, who returned my nod in recognition. She had seen what I had, and we could not speak to each other. I removed my sterile apparel and left the room, physically drained and emotionally numb.

As I slowly walked down the hallway, I knew that, in due time, Sue would finish drying the baby and wrap it in a soft blanket. She would then allow the mother to hold it and grieve, and the family physician on call would soon arrive and give words of comfort and reassurance. But, for me, I was emotionally spent and had nothing more to offer. No training in medical school had prepared me to witness something that, fortunately, very few in the world have seen, a moment of unforgettable, spine-tingling horror, that of a premature baby, a fetus, hopelessly struggling to live.

I slowly returned to my room and collapsed in the bed. Sleep would be a long time coming, if it ever did.

Chapter 6

THE CADAVER

I nherent in the training of medical school was learning to do things that were uncomfortable. While this could apply to much of medical education, the first and the most in-your-face task to deal with was Human Anatomy, a course which required the dissection a cadaver. A handful of my colleagues had already experienced this edgy exercise while in college and perhaps were a bit more at ease than I was. For most, though, it was certainly not something we looked forward to, rather, just another necessary step on the pathway to becoming a physician.

It's bad enough when you have to rip apart the corpse of someone you don't know. But can you imagine opening up the lid of the body container and discovering a carcass of a person you'd been acquainted with beforehand? I've read several reports of this actually happening. One case involved a medical student at Dartmouth Medical School in 1958, who was assigned to a cadaver that turned out to be his previous French professor. A second incident occurred in 1982 at the University of Alabama School of Medicine, when one

of the cadavers was the student's great aunt. In both instances, a sub-
stitute body was provided.

These rare cases aside, dissecting a cadaver still ranks way up
there in the listing of troublesome learning experiences. I'll never
forget that first day in human anatomy lab, way back in August 1973.

The dreaded semester began. All of those in my module—a
small grouping of medical students—huddled around a stainless steel
tank, which was roughly the shape of a large casket. The entire room
reeked with the unpleasant, tear-inducing odor of formaldehyde. After pulling open the top cover, which was split down the middle and
attached by hinges on the sides, the instructor turned a handle at the
foot of the tank, raising the body inch by inch. The other name for
the course, Gross Anatomy, seemed increasingly fitting. The corpse
slowly emerged, zombie-like, out of the preserving fluid, feeling more
like a horror movie than a class. We held our breaths in anticipation.
*Would the body be male? Female? Old? Young? Someone with mul-
tiple gunshot wounds? A famous movie star who decided to donate his
or her body to science?*

As a group, we sighed in disappointment as out from the tank
surfaced a very old, emaciated man, and it was clear that he'd had
some sort of protracted illness that led to his demise. Once the body
was fully exposed, the instructor explained that each of us would be
assigned in pairs to dissect a certain portion of the corpse, the first
being the chest and arm. Our required duty was to demonstrate the
important anatomical structures to the others in our module.

When our professor asked for volunteers to start the dissection process, I, along with another student—Nina—shot up our
hands, and we were selected. I was uneasy, at best, with being the
first to dive into the figurative abyss. But, at the same time, I wanted
to get it over and done with. Besides, since we were green medical
students, I selfishly had a modicum of hope that perhaps the professor would cut the first volunteers on our team a bit of slack. Once

the dissection schedule for the rest of the body was determined, the teacher made a few beginning cuts and showed us some of the basic structures, but from that point it was completely up to us.

The next day Nina and I met at an agreed-upon time to begin our dissection. Mimicking our professor, we slung open the lids of the container, allowing them to fall to the side of the tank with a loud *clang*, and we turned the handle that raised the body up. We had an array of instruments on a nearby tray, which included scalpels and forceps.

Once the squeamishness at making our first incisions was overcome, the trick was to dissect the tissues carefully away without cutting the vital structures. We had *Grant's Atlas of Anatomy* splayed out in front of us and from the numerous diagrams, knew exactly what we were supposed to see. *This was going to be a piece of cake,* I thought. *How could we fail?*

Little did I know.

For several nerve-wracking hours we delicately snipped, cut and spread the tissues with our instruments. To our growing dismay, most of the structures we sought to expose were elusive and seemed impossible to find. We knew that we would have to meet again and work on the cadaver before our group demonstration, but I was not optimistic that a repeat session would be any more fruitful. Hopeless was the only way I could describe how I felt, and I could already see a big fat "F" on my grade card for Human Anatomy.

Three days later, the moment arrived for the demonstration to our fellow students, and while there was some improvement after the second try, at least half of the nerves, blood vessels and muscles that we were supposed to make visible were still buried deep within the tissue of the cadaver.

A look of disgust slowly eclipsed on the teacher's face as he peered through his brown frame glasses and stared at our meager efforts, shaking his head in disgust. It was as if the professor could not comprehend the sheer scale of our incompetence. With no small measure of disdain, he grabbed the instruments himself and took to the corpse with the skill of a surgeon. In a manner of moments, he'd ripped away the fibrous and fatty tissue that stood in the way, making short work of the rest of the dissection. I breathed a sigh of relief as he demonstrated the anatomical features that our pathetic attempts had left concealed.

At that juncture, my part in the dissection nightmare was finished. I would get to stand back, smile, and be entertained by the discomfort of my fellow students over the next four months as our cadaver's insides were gradually fully exposed for all to see.

As it turned out, the dreaded "F" never found its way to my report card. We were given quizzes on each section, and my scores on the other students' dissections were good enough that I was able to get by. I did not have an "A" by any means, but that was okay with me. I'd have taken any score that would have kept me from ever having to take that course again.

While learning human anatomy was necessary to become a qualified physician, dissecting cadavers was, for the sensitive student, a difficult exercise to manage. As I look back, I realize that during that semester, we were constantly reminded of our own mortality; someday we—our bodies—would be corpses as well. While intellectually we knew that someday, in the distant future, we would die, the laying open of a human body by our own hands placed this stark, cold inevitability of death right in front of our faces.

Now, as I think back on the whole exercise that semester, there was much more to it than just being confronted with our own deaths. The body Nina and I worked on was once a real person who had a life full of experiences, friendships, and family relationships that were important to him.

One might guess that the cadaver we worked on back in

1973 was born sometime in the early 1900s. Perhaps he had an older brother who was a soldier in World War I, whom he would have greeted at the train station when his brother returned from the travails and horrors of war.

Conceivably, he loved barbershop quartets, and maybe he even sang in one, wearing a straw boater hat, with a red, white and blue hat band, as he crooned out patriotic songs. Could it be that his wife-to-be heard his soaring tenor voice, swooned and fell madly in love with him?

He likely would have had children sometime during the Roaring Twenties, an astonishing period of growth when radio, electricity, automobiles, telephones and motion pictures exploded into public awareness. I wonder if he bought and drove a Model T Ford, feeling the thrill of the wind in his face as he topped it out at the reckless speed of forty-five miles per hour? I suspect that, like most young men, he enjoyed sports, and he perhaps was a fan of Babe Ruth and the New York Yankees.

He and his family would have experienced the privations and hardships of the Great Depression, and if he lived in Oklahoma during the 30s, he would have also had to survive the devastation of the Dust Bowl. Perhaps he even made the migration to California with his fellow Okies, searching for a better life for his family. Then came Pearl Harbor and a second world war, when he likely recycled tin cans and was issued ration coupons. In the midst of these difficult times, he and his family might well have huddled around the radio on Saturday night, listening to the Jack Benny Show or Hank Williams on the Grand Ole Opry. One might guess, no matter where he lived, that he and his family experienced more-than-occasional times of hunger. Perhaps one of his young children might have died from the dread affliction of that time, dust pneumonia, or from some other bacterial infection easily cured today by antibiotics.

And so it goes . . .

The important thing to realize is that before he became this

corpse we studied, he had a vital life. He laughed, he loved, he cele-
brated childbirths, he beamed with pride as he watched his children
perform in school functions, he cried when his parents died, and he
gushed over his grandchildren and spoiled them as grandfathers often do.

As he approached his demise, he made the decision to donate
his body to medical science, so that in his death, he could help medical students become physicians. One thing is certain, he was a giving
man, one who wanted to help others.

So, the take-home message from my long-ago semester of cadaver dissection is this: It is important to savor all of the moments
of living, no matter how painful or joyous, exhilarating or wretched,
elevating or depressing. Each moment we live and breathe is sacred
beyond measure.

Even those times spent leaning over a formaldehyde-soaked
cadaver.

Chapter 7

MUCUS

Every top-notch emergency physician has a memory like an elephant and can recall specific cases that have occurred decades in the past. This ability, which is a close cousin to a photographic or eidetic memory, provides assistance in helping medical practitioners hone their skills. For this reason, any medical error made in the past, no matter how distant, is unlikely to be repeated.

The double-edged sword of this resource lies in the tendency to also remember the bad outcomes—no matter how many more times the physician has helped others escape the brink of death—and is analogous to a fish that has swallowed a hook. Life goes on, but the irritation lurks in your gut, just waiting to be regurgitated.

The humorous feature of this capacity to retain certain events occurs when someone on the hospital staff demonstrates a weakness of any kind. Of course, we in medicine try our best to hide these soft spots, preferring to project an image of invincibility.

Specific vulnerabilities vary from person to person. Revulsion to blood products is a common frailty, whether it's spewing from a wound, gurgling from the throat or pouring out of the rectum. For others, it can be an aversion to horrific odors, such as the rotten smell of partially digested food (my own personal weakness), the putrid stink of infectious diarrhea or the unpleasant bouquet of a recently opened abscess. Sometimes certain sounds can trigger the *I-gotta-get-outta-here* feeling, such as the revolting noise of persistent vomiting or the sucking sound that occurs when a drainage tube is placed in the stomach or the chest.

When this weakness is revealed, the unfortunate medical practitioner will be picked on and reminded of the incident *ad infinitum* by colleagues, much like pecking chickens do when a fine-feathered friend is wounded. No case demonstrates this more clearly than an experience I had with an x-ray tech named Sophie over thirty years ago. Like an elephant, I recall the event in fine detail.

One afternoon in the emergency department, I was in a room examining a patient when one of the EMTs knocked on the closed door. I cracked it open. "Yes?" I questioned.

"Doctor Conrad," she said, with a panicked look on her face. "The nurse wants you in room eight *right now.*"

Say no more, I thought as I excused myself from the patient and ran across the hall. Lying on the stretcher before me was an agitated, elderly woman in severe respiratory distress. The nurses had applied a non-rebreathing oxygen mask to her face, one which can deliver up to 100% oxygen. As I entered, I could hear a gurgling sound rattling in her throat.

"What's going on?" I asked the nurse.

"Eighty-seven year old female with a history of dementia—transfer from a nearby nursing home. She has had a cough and fever for the past three days, and just yesterday she was placed on the antibiotic Rocephin. This morning she began having difficulty breathing."

"Full code?" I asked, realizing that from her appearance that

she might require a tube to be placed in her airway and possible cardiopulmonary resuscitation.

"Yes."

"Oxygen saturation at the scene?"

"82%."

This is bad, I thought, knowing that the minimal desired level
was around 90%.

I looked at the monitor. Her pulse rate was one hundred-twenty, blood pressure 180/90, oxygen saturation—with the
mask—was now 92%.

"What's her temperature? I asked.

"103 degrees, axillary."

I performed a quick examination. She was confused, combative, advanced in years, and had severe difficulty breathing, which
was at least somewhat due to secretions—probably from pneumonia—partially occluding her airway. Putting on my stethoscope, I
listened to her chest and discovered she had loud rales—sounds of
fluid in the lungs—scattered throughout. Her abdomen was soft, flat
and non-tender.

Pulling off my stethoscope, I ordered, "Call respiratory and
laboratory to the room STAT. Please put her in restraints until she
gets a little more alert. I want an EKG and a portable chest x-ray done
now, and bring to the bedside a nasotracheal suction catheter to the
bedside, and make sure it's one with a trap." I knew if I didn't act
quickly to clear her airway, she could die.

Moments later the catheter arrived, and with the nurse holding her head as still as possible, I advanced the plastic tubing into her
right nostril, down the back of her throat and into her trachea—her
windpipe. I turned on the suction, causing a noxious, gurgling noise.
At once the tubing began to fill with a gruesome mixture of yellow,
green and brown mucus. The trap, which was attached inline to the
tubing, was gradually filling with the slimy mixture when I heard a
knock at the partially-opened door, and the x-ray technician, Sophie,

popped her head around the corner.

"X-ray," she announced as she directed her portable machine into the room.

No sooner had she passed the threshold of the door, the sickening odor of mucus and the revolting, slurping sound of suction slapped her across the face like a bullwhip. Her eyes bulged ever-so-slightly, and she retched, not just once, but repeatedly. As I stood between Sophie and the patient, I felt like I was surrounded by a symphony of grotesqueness, and I briefly closed my eyes and took a deep breath to center myself. When I glanced back toward the door, the x-ray machine was still there, but Sophie had vanished.

Turning my attention back to the patient, after the mucus had been suctioned from her throat, I was relieved to see that her breathing had improved dramatically, and her oxygen saturation had risen to 100%. Clearly, putting a tube in her airway to assist her breathing would not be necessary.

But where was Sophie?

Some time later, after Sophie had regained her composure, she returned to take the x-ray, which confirmed the diagnosis of pneumonia. Antibiotics were ordered, and the patient was admitted to ICU.

Thankfully, the grisly symphony had reached its conclusion.

As could be guessed, the chickens in the chicken yard soon commenced their attack, and Sophie was teased about this incident many times over the years. Of course, I was not innocent in that unrelenting pecking at her newly discovered wound, and when Sophie would arrive in the emergency department to take x-rays, I would invariably ask, "Hey Sophie, there's a man in room six who needs to be suctioned. Would you please take care of him?"

Sophie would always turn a bit red, screw up her face, and then she would object, exclaiming, "Doctor Conrad!" In spite of being repeatedly needled about the incident, I always suspected that she didn't mind, as she enjoyed a good laugh just as much as the rest of us. Besides, in emergency medicine, we've learned to recycle our humor. Why go to the trouble to come up with something new when you can reuse the same old material?

When Sophie took a position at a different hospital in the years to come, we all missed her.

Twenty years later I was making my rounds in the emergency department, when I pulled a chart from the "To Be Seen" rack. The chief complaint was "Fall—tailbone injury."

I picked up the chart and walked into the room. Much to my surprise, there sat Sophie.

Delighted, I said, "It's good to see you again. How are you?"

"Not well. I was standing on the toilet seat to put up some medications in the cabinet above it; I didn't want to take the chance my children might get into them. Somehow I lost my balance and fell on my bottom. My tailbone is killing me."

I asked, "Are you hurting anywhere else?"

"No."

"Didn't hit your head?"

"No."

"No pain in your neck, chest or abdomen?"

"No."

"Any chance of pregnancy?"

"I've had a hysterectomy."

"Good," I said. "X-rays, if necessary, will be safe. Let me take a look at you."

With that, my examination revealed exquisite tenderness and swelling over her coccyx—the tailbone. Her strength, sensation and reflexes were normal in her legs, and the rest of her exam was unremarkable.

"Sophie, I'm going to order some x-rays of your tailbone. The tech should be here shortly to take your films. But before I leave, may I ask you one more question?"

"Of course," she replied.

"There's a woman in room four who has a bad cough. Would you mind suctioning her before you go to x-ray?"

Sophie's eyes twinkled as she loudly laughed and gave her usual protest, "Doctor Conrad!"

I chuckled along with her before I left the room. Later, I found the x-rays to be normal, and she was released to go home with a prescription for pain.

In the years to come, she returned once again to work at my hospital, and to her chagrin, the first time I saw her, I posed the same question. As always, she laughed and halfheartedly pretended to object.

Do I have the memory of an elephant?

Of course, I do. Doesn't every top-notch emergency physician?

Chapter 8

SOMEONE HAS TO DO IT —
WHY DOES IT HAVE TO BE ME?

Work in the emergency department is not a run-of-the-mill job. The unfortunate truth is that most of us who work there are exposed to a daily barrage of offensive human secretions and substances, ranging from saliva, urine and blood, to vomit, pus and diarrhea.

Even worse is that some of these body fluids are contagious, and we would prefer not to be gifted with someone else's disease, much less take it home to share with our families. Sharing is caring, but not in emergency medicine, so we use precautions such as wearing gloves, masks and diligently scrubbing our work stations with alcohol or an antiseptic of some kind. Occasionally, though, we are caught off guard, and end up wallowing in infectious material.

Nevertheless, certain duties are expected of the emergency practitioner that most outsiders wouldn't do for all of the gold in Fort Knox. But, in emergency medicine, they're simply part of the job description. So, take this as fair warning: for those who have weak stomachs and get queasy at the thought of a hangnail, stop here.

Go on to the next chapter where things are likely to be a little mellower and less unpleasant.

We'll start off with something easy—body odor. The fact is, most folks who come to see me haven't had the chance to clean up, and that's completely understandable. It's called the emergency department for a reason, and when an unexpected crisis occurs, the patients are not expected to make themselves presentable beforehand. But a substantial number haven't had a bath in weeks, or maybe even months. So, the situation is even more odious than one would normally expect.

As I have mentioned in a previous writing, one of the great blessings I have inherited is a diminished sense of smell. Pity the poor chef, perfume mixer, or wine taster whose sniffer in on the fritz, but in the setting of the emergency department, this trait is greatly appreciated. One day, I went to see a man who was one of those 'no bath for two weeks' sort of guys. While in the examining room, even I got a bit green about the gills with the foulness of the odor emanating from him.

I left the room after the examination to write a few orders. A few minutes later, I heard the unmistakable sound of vomiting come from the room, and I discovered one of the nurses had gone to draw blood from him, and began throwing up in the trash can at his bedside. Yes, it was that bad.

Another unsavory task in the emergency department is the draining of abscesses. The only salvation in this situation occurs if the abscess is too large to simply incise and instead requires being opened in surgery. While collections of pus can occur anywhere, the most spectacular one I recall was on a man's lower back. It was huge, but not big enough to require a trip to the OR.

So, after injecting local anesthesia, I opened the area with an 11 blade scalpel – one with a pointed tip – and while applying gentle pressure the contents of the giant abscess exploded upward, almost hitting the ceiling. Mount Vesuvius and Old Faithful had nothing on this abscess, though I suspect neither of them smelled quite so putrid.

I still remember one of the nurses at the bedside saying, "Wow! Look at . . ." At that point the smell leaped like a grasshopper into her nostrils, and she left the room retching. Those who have a sensitive sense of smell should never work in the emergency department.

One thing I've observed over the years is that the novice nurse will lean forward during these procedures to take in all the action, no matter how repulsive, while the wiser, more experienced nurse has a face shield on and leans back as far as possible. No one enjoys wiping a glob of thick pus from their face, especially if it originated from someone else.

I still recall in my training a time when an unfortunate young man presented to our hospital with an empyema, a collection of pus in his lung. The treatment for this condition is to insert a plastic chest tube between the ribs into the space where the infection resides. Once placed, the tube is attached to suction and intravenous antibiotics are administered.

As a first year resident, I was pleased that my senior resident allowed me to put in the chest tube. The surgical tray was set up, and with an extra-long needle I anesthetized the skin and the area between his ribs. After an incision was made, using surgical forceps, I dissected the tissue up to the lining of the lung, and I inserted the tube with a satisfying *pop* into his chest cavity. Immediately pus under pressure exploded into the tube. My resident exclaimed, "Way to go, Gary!" and just after he spoke my name, the purulence from the tube rocketed into his open mouth. I had erred—I hadn't clamped the end of the tube prior to inserting it, and now my resident's face was beet-red as he coughed and sputtered with his mouth full of nasty yellow-green pus.

Immediately, he grabbed a nearby bottle of mouthwash and gargled and spat—gargled and spat—gargled and spat—so many times I lost count. After that experience, for some reason my senior resident and I didn't get along quite as well. One can only guess why.

Another procedure which is low on the list of enjoyable happenings is the draining of a thrombosed hemorrhoid, in other words, a hemorrhoid with a large clot in it. Most hemorrhoids, which are swollen veins in the rectum, aren't too bad, and the associated swelling and pain can easily be treated with stool softeners, sitz baths, steroid suppositories and pain medicine. But a thrombosed hemorrhoid requires drainage for the patient to get any modicum of relief.

The procedure for this is simple, but has to be done carefully. After laying the patient down on his stomach, the nurse has the thrilling duty of holding the butt cheeks apart so the physician can get to the bulging, blue-tinged mass perched like a vulture on the rectum. Everyone involved says a silent prayer that for lunch the patient didn't have beans, or, God forbid, sweet potatoes—known colloquially as "poot roots."

After numbing the area, a small incision is made, and the blood clot usually instantly protrudes from it. If some squeezing is necessary to remove the clot, watch out. I've seen them shoot out from the incision three to four feet—sometimes more. Of course, the nurse is never too pleased with you if the thick, bloody clump discharges from the hemorrhoid like a bullet fired from a gun and jumps onto his surgical scrubs.

If indeed it did, after an agonizing scream, he would immediately go to the sink, wipe the clot off and apply a liberal amount of disinfectant, and hope that the blood didn't soak through his scrubs onto his skin. Complete stain removal is very difficult, though, without using a good washing machine with liberal amounts of detergent and Clorox. It's not exactly a prelude to a romantic evening when the nurse returns home and his wife snuggles up to him and asks, "Hey, Honey, how'd you get that red splotch on your scrubs?"

If not totally offended by now, don't worry, there's more.

One of the most disliked problems the emergency staff has to deal with is constipation. Most of the time, this is a fairly easy problem to resolve. Between Milk of Magnesia, stool softeners, enemas, Dulcolax, and countless other laxatives, it's not too hard—literally—to get things moving along again, and this can all take place at home. But those with constipation who come to the emergency department are usually at their wit's end. They've tried everything, or so they think.

The classic age group with this problem is the elderly population. While many different things can cause constipation, such as a sedentary lifestyle, decreased fluid intake and certain medications, these are all issues that are common with the aged. Even Hippocrates once said, ". . . the intestines tend to become sluggish with age."

And so, the case might go something like this:

"Mr. Williams, I see on the chart that you're constipated. How old are you?"

"86."

"When was your last bowel movement?"

"Two weeks ago."

"Ever had this problem before?"

"Oh, yes, many times over the past few years. My last colonoscopy was two years ago, and it was fine."

"No vomiting, fever or abdominal pain?"

"No."

I take a look at the patient, and the examination is negative except for some distension in the lower abdomen. *Uh oh*, I think, *Houston, we have a problem.*

As I suspected, I discover on rectal exam a huge hard-as-a-rock fecal mass lounging in the rectum, preferring not to budge from its comfortable position in the recesses of the body. A simple enema won't help this problem, much as I'd like to defer this job to the nurses, and no medication given by mouth has a chance of working. There are only two things that might solve this issue: one, a nuclear weapon, or two, my index finger. And since the A-bomb does not qualify as standard emergency department equipment, it is up to me and my finger.

This procedure, to put it mildly, is not pleasant for either the patient or the doctor. The impaction has to be dug out, bit by bit, piece by piece. Once the concretion is loosened, eventually the patient is able to bear down and push it out, but not before agonizing moments where the physician feels like a miner breaking up rock wall with a pick ax. Once accomplished, though, I don't believe there's any patient that is more grateful. And, of course, every physician is grateful to have this onerous job completed.

One of the most graphic examples of this problem occurred, not in an elderly patient, but in an eight year old who arrived in our emergency department after gorging on sunflower seeds, eating them whole and not spitting out the shells. One of my colleagues discovered a huge sunflower seed amalgam in the boy's rectum, and, as described earlier, he had to break it up, seed by seed, clump by clump.

After hours of sweaty labor, success came suddenly when the nurse was walking the patient to the toilet. Unable to control himself, the sunflower seed bolus unexpectedly expelled from his rectum, covering the nurse's leg and foot with feces-coated seeds. Granted, it was a great victory, but at what cost? My understanding is that the nurse involved found seeds still stuck in her shoelaces after she returned home. I'm not sure what she eventually did with her shoes, but if I were in her shoes—pun intended—they would have gone into the incinerator.

Like any good writer, I've saved the best (worst?) for last, and that is the story of the tampon that has been interminably stuck in the vagina. Usually a woman is able to remove a lodged tampon herself, but every so often one gets pushed in a little too far, and she is unable to fetch it, no matter how hard she tries.

One late night I walked into a room, and a hint of a stench hung in the air. Remember, I have almost zero sense of smell, so it was probably much worse to anyone else. I glanced over at the nurse, whose face was expressionless. I looked harder and wondered: *Are her eyes bulging a bit?*

I introduced myself to the patient and said, "One of the nurses has informed me that you have a tampon stuck in your vagina."

"Well, I think I do."

"What do you mean?"

"Well, my last period was three weeks ago, and I believe I put one in then."

"You *think* you did?"

"Well, I'm not sure—I can't find it. But I'm a little worried. Something smells down there."

I had a concerned look on my face as I said, "The nurse will set you up for a pelvic exam, and we'll see what the problem is, okay?"

A short time later, I walked back into the room, sat on a stool in front of the pelvic table and inserted a speculum into her vagina. Immediately, an odor comparable to a dozen rotting animal carcasses surged forth. This was not a time to pause, so I acted quickly. I saw the sought after object, a balled-up blood-tinged, yellow-colored tampon, sitting deep inside her vagina, resting underneath her cervix. I grabbed some forceps, promptly removed it and placed it in a basin being held for me by the nurse. She wrinkled up her nose and promptly dashed out of the room, but before the repulsive article could be wrapped up and disposed of, the fetid smell soon penetrated every nook and cranny of the emergency department, and the entire place reeked.

As hard as it is to believe, other hospital personnel who were walking down the hall, as far as one hundred yards away, popped into the emergency department and asked, "Oh God, what's that smell? Did something die?"

The truth is they might not have been so far off. Yes, I've never smelled anything so putrid in my life—anything—as that rotting tampon. But even worse, the tampon was doubtlessly a cesspool of flourishing, toxic bacteria that if not removed could have led to septic shock, a disastrous and potentially deadly outcome. A greater emergency was averted, and that's a trade-off I'll take any day.

So, the next time when seeing a health care professional, whether socially or as a patient, take care to realize that their day, in all probability, has not been all peaches and cream. More than likely, they've been exposed to objectionable, sickening events, ones they hope to never experience again.

Yet, someone has to do their job, and all should be grateful that there are hardy souls such as doctors, nurses, and emergency medical personnel, that gladly—well, maybe not gladly—but at least willingly, take on such unpleasant responsibilities. And, if a red, brown, or yellow stain shows on their scrubs, have sympathy.

It might not be from ketchup, chocolate or mustard.

Chapter 9

DOCTOR DECKERT

B efore I began composing this chapter, questions churned inside my head: *What made Doctor Deckert such an astounding teacher? How could such a diminutive man paradoxically be such a colossus? Why do I still clearly remember his teachings after forty-four years?*

Even today, I recall Doctor Deckert as one of the most incredible men I have ever known. Any number of superlatives could be applied to him: stupendous, mind-boggling, extraordinary . . . But I am getting ahead of myself . . .

In 1973, after three years of undergraduate study at Oklahoma State University, I was accepted to the University of Oklahoma College of Medicine. Physicians often comment that the two best moments of medical school are when the acceptance letter arrives and the day one graduates. With that in mind, great trepidation followed me as I walked into the medical school halls of learning.

For the first year, the morning was packed with four hours of lectures on various topics, including Histology, Microbiology, and Human Behavior, among other meaty courses, teaching us a new complex language and the culture of medicine. In the afternoons we participated in Human Anatomy lab, Patient Contact—where we visited different physicians' offices and observed them in their practices—along with numerous other non-lecture activities.

With the necessary study time required to receive a passing grade in the courses, attending all of the lectures was nearly impossible, and thus medical students relied on what we affectionately called the "note group," where each lecture was recorded and transcribed by an assigned student. This arrangement took place in the days prior to the widespread use of computers, so a printed photocopy—not a computer file—was distributed to the other members of the note group, making attendance to each and every lecture unnecessary.

So, rather than sitting in the lecture hall listening to boring, stifling renditions on the Krebs cycle, with the professor vainly trying to convince us about how important this knowledge would be to us when we became physicians, we could spend our time studying the notes of previous lectures and make bona fide headway in our studies. As a result, the medical school lectures were usually sparsely attended, with one major exception, those presentations given by the psychiatrist, Doctor Gordon Harmon Deckert.

I'll never forget the first time I heard him speak. His talk to us was scheduled during the beginning week of medical school, when the lecture hall was still crowded with eager students, ready to hear the words of wisdom our teachers wished to instill into us, though I'm sad to say we often walked away disappointed. But Doctor Deckert was different. His reputation as a lecturer preceded him, and a hum of excitement filled the room as we awaited his grand entrance.

The large, theater-style lecture hall was a new, state of the art facility with around two hundred seats, but the space was not a setting conducive to a dramatic presentation. An over-sized projection screen was hung against the front wall, while three mammoth chalk- and whiteboards were situated below. A laboratory counter containing a stainless steel sink and a lone Bunsen burner acted as the podium. The locale was coldly institutional, dull and sterile, devoid of any pizzazz whatsoever.

In stark contrast, when Doctor Deckert made his entry, he oozed a sense of drama that literally filled the auditorium. Other professors shuffled up to the podium, faces down, glancing distractedly at their notes. Deckert paraded into the lecture hall with aplomb, staring us to silence with his stark, piercing blue eyes. When he arrived at the front of the hall, it became as quiet as an undiscovered tomb on Easter Island.

We wondered: *What the hell?*

Doctor Deckert continued to stare at our naïve, cherubic faces as he began, "Today, we are going to talk about your upcoming journey through medical school." He cleared his throat, raised his chin with an air of pomposity and continued, "Man inevitably is curious about himself. Inexorably, he strives to satisfy this curiosity. Sometimes, in his curiosity, he elects to that profession called medicine, and he becomes that easily recognized but poorly understood variety of Homo sapiens known as the medical doctor . . ."

As he continued his oration, I was certain that he had somehow missed his calling as a Shakespearean actor. His delivery style was unique and in sharp contrast to most of the other faculty, who somehow expected us to master an enormous amount of material, no matter how dull and monotonous the delivery.

In spite of the obvious grandeur, I must confess that Doctor Deckert reminded me of a leprechaun. I found it impossible to look at him without thinking of the leprechaun king in the Disney classic, *Darby O'Gill and the Little People*. Like the king, Doctor Deckert was somewhat portly and short in stature, though instead of the king's reddish-brown hair, he proudly sported closely-trimmed, straight white hair and distinctive, mutton-chop sideburns. He carried a regal, professional air about him, and he wore a nicely-fitted light grey, three-piece suit. His official title was Professor and Chairman, Department of Psychiatry and Behavioral Sciences, but as we soon discovered, he was much, much more. While his initials were GHD, it was rumored among the medical students that his middle name was actually Oscar, making his initials GOD.

I found myself entranced by his presentation style. He utilized all the skills of an Academy Award winning actor, and then some. His facial expressions turned on a dime; one minute he might be softly chuckling, the next he could be hysterically screaming, a moment later he would be red-faced and maniacally laughing, and before we could catch our breath, weeping inconsolably. We sat in awe before this force of nature, wondering what was going to happen next. Doctor Deckert was completely unpredictable, which made him the most interesting speaker I had ever heard—bar none.

Moreover, his speed of delivery and the emphasis of his oration never stayed constant. This, combined with his animated teaching style, hand waving and strutting about, jumping onto and sitting on the counter, even walking on the counter when he wanted to make a point, made the whole presentation stupefying. The best way to describe the lecture was as a hologram, a multi-dimensional aural and visual experience that surrounded and enveloped the listener. Sometimes I halfway expected him to rise in the air above us, like Peter Pan, with a subsequent cadence of *oohs* and *aahs* cascading from the students below him. While such a spectacular event never happened, I was certain Doctor Deckert felt his material was important, and he wanted desperately for us to understand and apply the concepts to our patients when we became clinicians. So, with that purpose in mind, he was willing to do anything to keep us engaged.

And keep us engaged he did.

As the year passed, each lecture became crammed with more students than the one before. At times, as they say in the theater business, it was SRO (Standing Room Only). I suspected that once the word got out, other outlying students and interlopers crashed the party just so they could hear the words of GOD. I recall my room-mate and I arriving at the auditorium early, not only to be certain we each got a seat, but also to get the full effect of his speeches. We sat on the front row, and my hair stood on end from the volume of air that would blast forth from his massive, resonant throat, and I swear I could see saliva spraying out of his mouth like a geyser when the volume of his voice exploded to rock-concert levels.

Not only was Doctor Deckert a charismatic lecturer, also his presentations also represented a masterful synthesis of the histo-ry of psychiatry. Over the year that he lectured us, he introduced classical Freudian theory, as well as Erikson's psychosocial stages of development, Piaget's theory of cognitive development, Kohlberg's moral development theory, and so on. At the same time, he provided a practical clinical introduction to the mental status examination and specific criteria for psychiatric diagnoses and treatments.

While all of his presentations were memorable, several stood out as truly exceptional. For these clinical vignettes, Deckert would act the role of both himself and the patient, creating a visual portrait stronger than mere words ever could. In one of those talks, Doctor Deckert related how he was asked to help with a schizophrenic pa-tient who was an inpatient at a psychiatric institution. Deckert had been informed that the patient sat unmoving in a corner of his room, stared straight ahead and mumbled repeatedly, "It's a long way doon to baboon foon," or other rhyming gibberish. Attempts to converse with him had been futile, and the patient never communicated in any way with the outside world.

The patient was a young man in his mid 20s, pale, with oily, straight black hair that hung across his eyes. Upon first meeting him, as expected, the patient uttered to Deckert, "It's a long way doon to baboon foon."

Deckert leaned over and answered, "And on your way up, many a bitter cup you must sup."

At that point, a look of recognition crossed the patient's face and he excitedly said, "Hey Doc, you speak schizo!"

From that time on, the patient began to engage with others. Doctor Deckert knew that to communicate with those having an altered perception of reality, the caregiver must temporarily enter that state of consciousness. That story left an indelible mark on me, and on all who heard it.

Another anecdote involved a medical student with a suspected conversion disorder. Also called a functional neurological symptom disorder, the Mayo Clinic defines it as "a condition in which you show psychological stress in physical ways." In conversion disorder, the symptom is symbolic of the stress, as compared to a psychosomatic illness, where the symptom is *not* symbolic. As the story went, Doctor Deckert was asked to see a medical student who complained that he couldn't use his right arm. His clinical workup by a neurologist was completely normal, so Deckert was asked to evaluate him for a possible psychiatric cause. Doctor Deckert re-enacted the encounter, and he demonstrated how the medical student stiffly walked into his office wearing a starched white medical jacket, a white shirt with a conservative blue, paisley tie. Deckert immediately noticed that his right arm was uselessly dangling at his side, but the fist was clenched, and he pointed out to us that in a true paralysis, the hand should have been limp and open. As Deckert interviewed him, he discovered that the patient's father was a surgeon who wanted the son to follow in his footsteps. After completing his evaluation, Deckert believed that the student's conflict had become manifested as a useless right arm. After all, how could he become a surgeon if his dominant arm couldn't function? Perhaps he didn't want to be a surgeon? Maybe he didn't even want to be a doctor?

As Deckert explored this conflict with the medical student, in a flash the young man realized that he didn't have to follow his father's wishes, and that his "paralysis" was likely a direct result of this dissonance. Deckert played the role of the student, looking down at his arm as he began to open and close his hand. "Oh my God, I can move it again," Deckert said as he role-played the young man, real tears forming in Deckert's eyes. We sat enthralled, convinced we had witnessed the depiction of a miracle.

Another of Deckert's astounding presentations was on the psychological journey of physicians, a lecture he gave on a number of occasions, not only to medical students, but also to their fathers and mothers on Parent's Day. After my unequivocal recommendation, my parents both decided to attend, and they were excited about seeing the famed Doctor Deckert. All was going well until one dramatic moment, when Deckert roughly cleared his throat, filling his mouth with saliva and mucus. He then glared at the audience, who were stunned to silence. At that point, he spit the wet glob into his hand, and before the crowd could react, he put his mouth down to his palm and proceeded to lick it up. Audible groaning went up from the audience, sickened by what they had witnessed.

Deckert, who seemed to be enjoying the discomfort of those in attendance, looked up from his slimy snack and said, "You see, ladies and gentlemen, as long as secretions, such as saliva, urine, and feces, stay in the body, they are somewhat acceptable. When they leave the body, they become filthy and vile. This is what your son or daughter will be exposed to in their years in medical school."

Our parents sat in their chairs in stunned silence, and one could have heard a piece of lint as it floated down and touched the floor. No doubt, each of them was wondering what in heaven's name their child was about to go through, and was it *really* a good idea to commit all of their financial resources to a process that could change their progeny forever? And perhaps not in a good way?

As a footnote to this story, recently I told my father that I was writing a chapter about Doctor Deckert for my new book, and he exclaimed, "I still remember the speech he gave to us. He was one of the most dynamic speakers I have ever heard!" To me, it speaks volumes that Dad would recall Deckert's talk from forty-four years ago with such clarity. But that was Doctor Deckert: simply unforgettable.

Other pearls of wisdom transcribed by me and my colleagues from Doctor Deckert's mesmerizing lectures:

"The fantasy is not the fact; the feeling is not the act."

"You are always a physician, but not only a physician."

"A man who does not know how he feels can never be free; and incidentally he is a man especially vulnerable to disease."

"Man inevitably is curious about himself. Inexorably he strives to satisfy this curiosity. Sometimes, in his curiosity, when he needs an answer, but when he finds he doesn't like what he discovers, he becomes angry."

"Life is a series of 'hello, thank you, you're welcome and good-bye.' Skip any of those steps and one will become stuck psychologically."

"The patient declares the disease, not the physician."

"That which is labeled disease is always multiply determined."

"To know the disease is to know the patient, to know the patient is to know the man, and to know the man is to know his emotions."

"Fear quickens the heart, but anxiety tears at the gut."

"Destructive and diseased is the man who is angry and knows it not."

Without any question whatsoever, I can say that Doctor Deckert was much more than a colossus. He had a profound influence on me, more than any other professor or clinician in all of my years of medical school, and I have no doubt he had a similar effect on others over his forty-three years of teaching medical students. While I learned many things from him, perhaps the most consequential point was the critical importance of the mind in illness. The interaction that takes place between mind and body is so innate and intertwined that the two can never be separated from each other.

So, Doctor Gordon Harmon Deckert—GHD, not GOD—

I feel most blessed that I was lucky enough to have had you as my teacher. Like thousands of other medical students you taught, I will never forget you.

Thank you, Doctor Deckert.

Chapter 10

THE TOO-TIGHT SUIT

Appearance is everything, or so we're told.

For as long as I can remember, one of the primary foci of our American society has been appearance. If we don't look good, well, we might as well slime around in the dirt like a lowly snake, shunned by all.

The diametric opposite to our American fascination with riveting beauty is nursing homes. While there is a unique charm to aging, growing older goes against the grain of our national obsession with youth and attractiveness. Think about it. Has there ever been a soap opera about love and romance in a nursing home?

The court date was today, and after a restless night's sleep, I was already dreading giving my testimony. A physician associate (PA) in our emergency department was being sued for missing a case of appendicitis, which eventually led to the appendix rupturing. The post-operative course was uncomplicated, and the patient did well. But, that didn't matter, as according to the plaintiff and her attorney, the diagnosis *should* have been made.

I was surprised the lawsuit had gone this far, since most such actions are either dropped or settled long before they get to court. The time when this emergency visit occurred was well before the routine use of CAT (computerized axial tomography) scans to diagnose appendicitis, and so emergency providers did the best they could by utilizing the history, physical, and laboratory evaluation. Early in the course of appendicitis, though, even with the modern use of CAT scan technology, making a definitive diagnosis can be difficult, and that's why an occasional case will be missed. In this particular incident, I concluded it was just too soon in the progression of the illness to make a definitive diagnosis, and I agreed to testify on the PA's behalf.

I had previously been told by the defense attorney that I would be notified sometime in the afternoon when my testimony was needed, so that left the morning free to run a number of overdue errands. After donning my blue jeans and an old tee-shirt, I hung my dress clothes up in my turquoise-green Honda Accord and went about my business. I attached my beeper to my belt, for in that day and age, as hard as it is to fathom now, no one carried cell phones.

As I drove away from my home that morning, I was aware that appearances—*especially* in a court of law—are critically important, and that attorneys routinely inform people appearing in court never to wear anything that draws attention to themselves, such as gaudy, expensive jewelry or watches. A defendant taking the stand sporting a Rolex watch or a big, sparkling diamond ring might as well prepare to pay up, because the jury will view him or her as a fat cat with lots of money to burn, no matter the merits of the case.

Like jewelry, if the defendant happens to own a $3,500 Italian-made Ermenegildo Zegna suit that fits like a glove and looks like a million dollars, it might be best to keep it in the closet and wear the $300 suit purchased at a local department store. Also, it's probably best that a woman not wear a short dress that will require constant tugging at, or a low cut dress that might reveal a little too much. Jurors, consciously or subconsciously, frown on such a deportment of wealth or sexuality in the courtroom. Nor is it a good idea to show up with purple-dyed hair or wearing low hanging pants that reminds the juror of a down-and-out homeless person. Facial piercings should be removed beforehand—and facial tattoos covered—or one might as well settle the case beforehand, as it would be nearly impossible to win, given the conservative nature of many jurors.

In summary, the overriding rule is this: dress simply, don't be ostentatious, and don't give the jury any reason to decide against you based on appearance. After all, the courtroom is not a nursing home, where we tolerate appearances that are somewhat less than appealing, or a bar, where one might intend to invite temptation.

In retrospect, how I wish I had listened to my own advice.

Sometime after twelve noon my beeper squealed out, and when I glanced at it, I recognized the phone number of the attorney. He had previously informed me that when he paged me, I had thirty minutes before my time on the stand.

Fifteen minutes later, I pulled my car into a parking area in front of the stately, granite county courthouse and headed inside, duffel bag, suit, dress shirt and tie in hand. When I located the correct courtroom, I scurried to the nearest restroom to change my clothes.

Finding one, I hung up my suit and tie on a hanger, and I began to change. When I started to put on my suit, I was shocked to discover: *Oh, God, it's not just small—it's almost unwearable.*

Then, with a start, I realized I had bought this suit a few months after I was divorced, when I had lost around fifteen pounds. In the interim, I hadn't worn the suit again, and I had regained all that weight and then some.

I glanced at my watch. I had to be in the courtroom in five minutes. There was no other option; I had to find a way to cram myself into the get up that now seemed better suited—pun intended—

for a Munchkin. I first squeezed into my pants, only to discover that I was a solid three inches short of being able to button it up. I put on my belt and cinched it as tight as I was capable of doing, but there was still a one-inch gap, and I was unable to completely pull up my zipper.

Then came the shirt—no way could I button up the collar without asphyxiating myself. So, I put on my conservative blue-patterned tie and cinched it around my neck as tight as my pants were drawn around my waist. I looked at my face in the mirror; it was red and puffy, and I could barely breathe. Putting on my dress coat was at least as much of a disaster. I could barely squeeze into it, and my arms awkwardly stuck out to the side.

When I glanced again at the mirror, I had the distinct feeling I was not looking at myself, but rather, at a human version of the Pillsbury Doughboy, minus the lovability and cuteness. I looked terrible, and that's being generous.

I stuffed my clothes into the duffel bag, then waddled, much like a penguin, into the courtroom and took my seat. The defense attorney nodded at me as I entered, and I noticed a look of concern on his face. I was certain he knew there was a problem, but did anyone else?

Shortly afterward, I was called to the witness stand, and I stumbled up, hoping that my underwear was not showing through the gap in the front of my pants. Sweating profusely, I slowly sat down, fingers crossed, praying to whatever clothing gods who might be listening, that my pants wouldn't split down the back with a distinctive ripping sound. How relieved I was when I didn't hear the fabric tearing.

The plaintiff's attorney had a slight, knowing smile on his face as he strutted up to the stand like a matador walking into a bullring. I was certain he instinctively sensed my weakened condition, and he moved in for the kill, much akin to a shark circling his prey. And there I was, floating on top of the water, waiting for the strike of his razor-sharp teeth and the feel of his powerful jaws squeezing the breath out of me.

And strike he did, quickly and without mercy. I was immediately peppered by a kaleidoscope of probing questions, and I felt like Rocky Balboa, dodging blow after blow, though, unfortunately—like Rocky—most found their mark. I somehow croaked out breathless answers as my constricting tie squeezed my voice box, and my hoarseness increased as the testimony went on. With the tightness of my collar, I was certain that I could feel the distension of my jugular veins. I wondered: *Could the lawyer see it as well?*

While being questioned, I wondered why there was all this jockeying for position and sideways approaches to the real facts. *Why not just go right for the truth?* But, unfortunately, such is not the nature of the courtroom, where well-disguised smokescreens, gross deceptions, and, in general, being a jerk, are often the *modus operandi* of the opposing attorney.

After what seemed like forever, but was actually only about an hour of sheer torture, my testimony and I were finished. The plaintiff's attorney had a smirk on his face as he sat down, as he knew I had been mortally wounded and left for dead, floating in a blood-tinged sea some call a courtroom. I answered a few easy questions from the defendant's lawyer, who did his best to verbally patch up my gaping wounds, though clearly, at that point, the damage was already done.

When the judge dismissed me, I stood and once again waddled, arms still sticking out from my sides, back to my courtroom seat, wishing that I could somehow remove my suit and put my street clothes on without being noticed.

At the first recess, I vanished from sight, never to be seen in that courtroom again.

The next day I was working in the emergency department when I discovered that the verdict had returned in favor of the plaintiff. The settlement was not exorbitant, but it was a loss all the same.

I couldn't help but feel badly for the PA.

Life goes on, and soon enough all of this drama would be neatly tucked away into the innermost parts of my mind. I wondered, though, if things might have gone differently had I coolly walked into the courtroom, sat comfortably at the stand, and in a normal tone of voice, smoothly explained my position.

That question will never be answered.

In lawsuits, just as our culture has taught us in so many other venues, appearance *is* everything.

Chapter 11

EGG ON MY FACE

My third year of medical school kept me as busy as a leg of a flea-infested dog, and the chances for personal moments were about as rare as a nun wearing a miniskirt. Any medical student might as well forget having the opportunity to even look in a mirror. Most have a chance to do so only twice a day, once in the morning at four a.m. when getting ready for a busy day at the hospital, and around ten p.m. when preparing to go to bed. When those moments came that I could actually take a quick peek at myself, I wished that those swollen, lack-of-sleep purple bags under my eyes would go away. Alas, they only worsened as medical school progressed.

I remember one particular summer morning when I was entrenched in the surgery rotation. While at breakfast, as I shoved some hastily prepared scrambled eggs and buttered toast into my mouth, I thought about my schedule for the day. I expected it would go something like this: after arriving at the hospital at five a.m., I would make visits to all of my patients, check their vital signs, review their laboratory results, change their dressings and make sure they were more alive than dead. Next would come six a.m. rounds, when I would report to my surgical team on the progress of my patients. Afterward, I would have to assist in surgery, attend lectures given by the faculty, and take care of any and all problems that reared their ugly heads while I was laboring at the hospital, and usually there were many. After evening rounds and taking care of any last-second duties, I was spent, and I would limp back home, dazed and exhausted.

Already, while rushing to finish breakfast, I was in dread-mode. After pausing for a moment to get my bearings, I dashed out the front door into the cool morning air.

Once I entered the hospital, a maelstrom even worse than usual engulfed me as I scurried around and frantically attempted to accomplish my required chores. Later, I was grilled by the intern and resident during rounds, mercilessly questioned by the surgeon in the operating room while I was straining to hold retractors for hours-on-end, and hassled by the nurses who seemed to believe that I, along with each and every medical student who walked the temples of healing, was about as qualified to be a doctor as the proverbial village idiot.

During one of the required lectures for the medical students, a crusty, steely-eyed surgeon who was convinced that no one on God's green earth really needed a gallbladder, peppered me with misleading questions, and, naturally, I knew answers to very few of them. By the time I crawled home at ten p.m., I was a shattered remnant of what I had been when the day started. I was hungry, beaten down, degraded and felt as low as a gopher on a quest to find the center of the earth.

After arriving home, I sat down, stupefied, and stared at the wall for an indeterminable period of time, wondering why in the hell I allowed myself to be subjected to such abuse. I finally forced myself to stand and wearily stumbled into the kitchen, where I prepared a quick meal of Hamburger Helper. Yes, I know what you're thinking;

but this was in the days before I became a pescaterian – one who eats
fish but no other meats. Close to collapsing and feeling like a geri-
atric patient who had no balance, I staggered to the bathroom and,
as I was getting ready to brush my teeth, I caught a look at myself in
the mirror.

Aside from the undisguisable fatigue and bloodshot eyes—
and, of course, the purple bags under my eyes—much to my surprise,
a gigantic glob of yellow-white egg was stuck in my moustache, hanging just above my right upper lip. It was speckled with black pepper
and was large enough to have kept a hungry person from starving. I
grimaced at the sight.

I pondered: *Why did no one tell me? How many of my colleagues saw the nutritious morsel perched there, yet didn't say anything?*
I imagined them snickering as I passed, saying, "Oh my God, did you
see that egg in Conrad's moustache? I wonder if he might have some
sausage that fell into his front shirt pocket? Maybe a hunk of French
toast stuck in his teeth?"

*And what about all the patients I had seen that day? Had they
decided not to tell me in order to spare my feelings, or did they guffaw
along with the nursing staff once I left their room?*

Of course, the surgeon in the operating room would not have
seen the colorful, congealed fragment because my face was covered
with a mask. But as my mind ran away with itself, I speculated that
maybe, just maybe, the surgery lecturer had spied the yolky mass of
egg from his podium, and that was why he decided to interrogate me
and make me talk, hoping the gummy glob would flip out and land
on the neck of the student sitting in front of me.

I will never know the answers to these questions, but, for the
moment, I was humiliated.

Literally and figuratively, I had egg on my face.

Chapter 12

INTENTION

Sometimes the people we hurt the most are the ones we love the most.

One day I was notified that an ambulance was on its way to the emergency department with an eighty-five year old man who'd been badly injured in a motor vehicle accident. He was a seat-belted passenger in the front seat of a car being driven by his wife. She pulled into an intersection, and when she failed to see and yield to another car, their vehicle was hit and T-boned, the passenger side of the car and her husband taking the brunt of the force.

After his arrival and my evaluation, I discovered he'd sustained multisystem injuries and needed to be transferred to a trauma center. I was concerned that for someone his age, the severe trauma inflicted by this accident could be fatal. Fortunately, his wife had only suffered minor injuries, and she was in the fast track of the emergency department, the area where non-urgent problems were treated.

After I had transferred her gravely-ill husband, I went to talk to the stricken woman, an anxious white-haired woman who appeared to be in her eighties. She was sitting in her examination room as I approached.

"Mrs. Smith?" I questioned.

"Yes. How is my husband?" she asked, her voice trembling slightly.

I wished I could find a way to sugarcoat the situation, but I had to be honest with her. I softly replied, "He's in critical condition."

"Where is he?" she said, as she started to stand.

"He is in an ambulance en route to the trauma center. I'm sorry you weren't able to see him before he was transferred."

"Will he . . . live?" she stammered out as she sat back down.

I solemnly answered, "I don't know."

Hearing my words, tears began to form in her eyes, and she whispered, "I believe I've killed my husband."

I tried to reassure her. "All of us make mistakes. Everyone. What's important is your intention. I know you did not want your husband to be injured."

"Of course, I didn't. But I believe I've killed my husband."

Nothing I could say could reassure her. After all, she was in danger of losing her life partner, just because of a moment of inattentiveness. Once her evaluation was completed, she immediately left with her family to drive to the trauma center. Her husband died a short time later.

Upon hearing the news of the man's death, like any concerned emergency physician, the wheels began turning in my mind, and I wondered: *Is there any action I could have taken that might have saved his life? Should I have done this? Should I have done that?*

In the days to come, I repeatedly processed and analyzed the decisions I made that fateful day. "What ifs" can plague physicians on cases that end in a bad outcome, and the associated feeling of remorse—no matter how good the care was—can continue for a while.

As I think deeply about critical decisions, the truth is that we make the best choices we can at a particular moment in time.

Whether an outcome would change as a result of a different action is often impossible to predict. Retrospect is always clear. Sometimes bad things happen—they just do—no matter the efforts one makes to change the outcome for the better.

I hope the patient's wife someday understands that intention is everything, and I pray that she can somehow find a way to forgive herself. Like physicians—and everyone else in the world—she is only human.

Life must go on.

No one is perfect.

Chapter 13

THE HEART ATTACK

A busy stint in the emergency department was effectively taking a pick ax to my usually calm state of mind, and I was just a few hours into a fifteen-hour shift, which lasted from six in the evening until nine in the morning. In a contemporary setting, laboring in such a frantic workplace for such a long stretch of time would be considered ludicrous, perhaps even dangerous. But this was years ago, when men were men and women were women, and health care providers were expected to gut it out no matter the circumstances. In hindsight, I wonder why John Wayne posters weren't placed at strategic locations to prod us onward to deal with the impossible. No bed of roses shifts for us, no cake walks, no strolling barefoot through fields of clover. As the Duke would say, with his typical western drawl, "When the going gets tough, the tough get going, so saddle up and keep movin', Pilgrim."

I was scampering from room to room, when one of the nurses informed me, "Doctor Conrad, a male with chest pain has just been checked into room four."

"How old is he?" I asked.

"Seventeen."

Oh brother, I thought to myself. *The chances of anything seriously wrong with this kid are about as rare as a squirrel that hates nuts. Why, of all times, when I'm completely overwhelmed, did he choose to come in tonight?*

"Okay," I grumbled. "Go ahead and get an EKG, and I'll see him in a few minutes."

Later, when I popped out of a nearby room, one that contained a moaning, hysterical patient with abdominal pain, the nurse sprinted up and stuck the EKG in my face. I could tell by the nervous look on her face that something was amiss.

"Oh, shit," I muttered under my breath as I examined the EKG, "Tombstones—an acute anterior MI. Have you started an IV yet?"

"We're working on it," she said.

For those who are naïve to emergency medical terminology, tombstones are what we call an EKG pattern that looks like the gravestones one might see in an old cemetery. They're indicative both of a heart attack and the eventual destination of the patient if the physician and nurses don't act fast.

I dashed for the patient's room, and just before I arrived, I heard a yell erupt from the doorway, "We need Doctor Conrad—*now*!

Running through the door, I discovered a sandy-haired, morbidly obese white male lying on the stretcher, completely unresponsive. The nursing personnel had already started basic life support (BLS) by breathing for the patient with a ventilation bag and performing chest compressions. I glanced up at the monitor and was shocked to discover ventricular fibrillation, uncoordinated contractions of the ventricles of the heart. If not corrected promptly, the rhythm could degenerate into asystole—flatline—which has an extremely high mortality rate.

"Apply the conductive gel pads," I said to the paramedic who had just entered the room. "Get the defibrillator here—STAT." In seconds, the electrical lifesaver was at the bedside, and I set it to 360 joules, unsynchronized. I applied the paddles atop the pads, pressing them firmly to the chest.

"All clear?" I questioned. With that, BLS was stopped, and I repeated, "All clear?" After making sure no one was touching the patient or leaning on the table, I pushed the buttons simultaneously on the paddles.

The patient's body lurched with the shock, and I quickly looked up at the monitor. After a few seconds of flatline, we all held our collective breaths, then suddenly his heart regained a normal rhythm, and he started to breathe again. Assuming he continued to improve, I decided that putting a tube into his airway would not be necessary. Aside from being obese, his examination was unremarkable.

"Get some vital signs," I ordered, "and let's put two large bore IVs in him. Do a repeat EKG and put him on oxygen at two liters/ minute via nasal cannula, draw a rainbow and call for a STAT portable chest x-ray. I want 100 mg of lidocaine given IV STAT, and start a drip at 2 milligrams per minute."

I hurried to the desk and phoned the cardiologist on call, who happened to be in the hospital. He promised he would come immediately.

I returned to the room and found the patient more alert. His vital sign were stable.

"Doc," he mumbled when he saw me, "my chest is killing me." *Indeed*, I thought, *it almost did*.

"You've had a heart attack," I informed him. "Soon the cardiologist will be here, and you'll be going to the cath lab to reopen the blocked artery in your heart. But for now, we'll get something for your pain."

To the nurse, I requested, "Please give him 324 milligrams of baby aspirin, 0.4 milligrams of sublingual nitroglycerin, and 4 milligrams of morphine IV. Any family members here yet?"

"No," the nurse replied.

At that moment, the cardiologist arrived along with the cath lab personnel, and the patient was whisked away.

How I wish I could have taken a short break after this major adrenaline rush, but the exam rooms were full, fifteen patients were holding in the waiting area, and, in spite of copious doses of pain medications, the patient I'd seen earlier with abdominal pain continued to moan.

Afterward, when I finally had a second to think about it, I couldn't wrap my mind around what had just happened. *Did the impossible really take place? A seventeen-year-old with an acute myocardial infarction?*

Now, about that abdominal pain . . .

Later that night I learned that the young man had a complete occlusion of his left anterior descending artery, a condition commonly called a "widow maker." The cardiologist had put in a stent, opening the artery so blood could flow through it again, and, as a result, the patient's life was saved. The rest of his hospital course was uneventful, and he was discharged several days later without further complications.

One might guess that the story ended here. Job well done—a life saved. But apparently, the message delivered to the young man by his near-death experience was not, shall we say, *taken to heart.* To my chagrin, around two weeks later, one of the nurses happened to see the patient dining at a Burger King, and stacked high on a tray in front of him were several orders of French fries and hamburgers. Obviously, the heart attack had not changed his dietary habits, and I could only predict that sometime in the future, sooner or later, we would see him again, and perhaps next time he might not be so lucky.

As I reflect on this critical event, I feel more than a little sad. In the '80s, the time when this heart attack occurred, the role of proper nutrition in the prevention of cardiovascular disease was not emphasized. While I believe health care professionals perform better now in preventive care than we did in the past, I'm not sure that much has really changed. Patients continue to indulge in unhealthy practices even with all the attention paid to developing good habits for food choices and the advantages of exercise.

But it's not just the patients who've been responsible for making poor health decisions. Consider for a moment some of the artery-congealing food typically served in hospitals. Fried chicken? Mashed potatoes slathered with gravy? Margarine? Onion rings? Bacon and sausage? Much of the time hospital fare is no healthier than what's found in a fast food joint, which is why I refuse to eat at the hospital. Why would I want to participate in the construction of a blockage in my own coronary arteries? For my safety and well-being, I bring my lunch when I venture to the hospital to work.

Another underlying problem is that hospitals mainly generate income when disease is treated, not prevented. So, what is the motivation to change? Certainly, institutionally speaking, there is not a financial one.

All these things considered, what about self-responsibility? I am absolutely certain that if I had a cardiac event, I would do all I could to avoid another one. I would carefully assess my diet, my exercise program, and, believing strongly in the mind-body connection, look at deepening my meditation practice and consider stress reduction. It's a sad fact that the most common time to have a heart attack is Monday morning between four and ten a.m., coincidentally when most are preparing to return to the pressure-packed environment of the workplace after a having a restful weekend off.

I believe that the way our healthcare system operates has to be fundamentally altered for any significant long-term impact to be made. People must sense the urgency to develop good health habits and consistently follow them. Also, we must always remember that we are ultimately responsible for our own wellbeing, not a hospital or someone who wears a long, white coat with a stethoscope around his or her neck.

Prevention and self-empowerment are the keys to good health. That two pronged approach, combined with effective interventions when medical crises happen to occur, gives a patient the best opportunity to live a long and healthy life.

Chapter 14

NO WORDS TO SAY

F ew events in emergency medicine make physicians more apprehensive than obstetrics; too many things can go wrong. First of all, the inherent problem exists that many pregnant women who present themselves to the emergency department have had no prenatal care. As a result, many situations that could have been resolved easily, if recognized and treated earlier, are left to grow unabated, like the slow, inexorable, ticking of a time bomb.

The list of treatable problems is lengthy, but one of the more common ones is pregnancy-induced diabetes, which can cause excessive birth weight and lead to difficulty delivering an oversized infant. Another condition is pre-eclampsia, an affliction of pregnancy typified by high blood pressure and protein in the urine, which increases the chance of bad outcomes for both mother and baby. Left untreated, this could eventually result in seizures and then is known as eclampsia.

What about the difficulties of the baby's delivery? A feared problem is the dreaded shoulder dystocia, which occurs when the shoulders fail to emerge promptly after the fetal head. This can result in death if the baby is not promptly delivered, as the life-sustaining umbilical cord is crushed within the birth canal, stopping the flow of blood and oxygen to the infant. And what if a patient arrives at the emergency department already in labor and the emergency physician finds one or two feet dangling outside of the vagina? Like the shoulder dystocia, a breech presentation can lead to an infant's demise simply because the umbilical cord is compressed while the head is stuck in the pelvis.

While emergency physicians do all that they can, these situations are challenging even for experienced doctors who are specialists in obstetrics, and no matter how quickly the obstetrician is able to arrive, it might still be too late to save the infant.

But even when a mother-to-be has been given adequate pre-natal care, bad things can still take place, as demonstrated by a nightmarish experience that happened during my initial year of training after medical school.

As a first-year family practice resident, I loved delivering babies, and I never minded being up in the wee hours of the night, since the blessed event nearly always brings great joy, not only to the patient and her family, but also to the attending doctor. Who could not be blissfully delighted to hand over a pink, screaming, wrapped-in-a-blanket, bundle of joy to a mother crying tears of happiness? *Welcome to the world, little one,* I would think with a smile on my face.

The hospital where I trained was located a few hours north of the Mexican border. More than a few women who were citizens of our southern neighbor wanted their babies to be born in that hospital so that their offspring would be lawful citizens of the United States of America. Many received prenatal care at the hospital or nearby clinics, as everyone concerned wanted a healthy baby, regardless of the social circumstances.

One wintry night, when I was taking call for obstetrics, I was beeped from my duties on the ward to report to labor and delivery. As I came through the doors into the labor area, the clerk sitting at the desk said, "You're wanted in room seven. A woman just presented in active labor."

"Okay," I answered as I hurried into the delivery suite. As I entered, the nurse assigned to the room was performing a vaginal examination on an anxious-appearing, Hispanic woman.

The middle-aged, graying nurse had a concerned look on her face as she said, "This is a twenty-five-year-old, gravida three, para two, Hispanic female, term by dates and in active labor. Her name is Maria Hernandez, and she was last seen in our clinic five days ago. Her checkup then was normal."

The patient looked over at us as she heard her name mentioned.

"Her third pregnancy and she has two living children?" I confirmed.

"Of course," she said. She pulled me to the side and whispered, "Her cervix is completely dilated, one-hundred percent effaced and at 1+ station, so she's ready to deliver. You should know, though, that there are no fetal heart tones, and the baby's head doesn't feel normal."

"Do you think we should call the chief resident to perform an emergent C-section?" I questioned.

"Doctor," she whispered with a tired voice, "you can do what you like, but . . . I'm sure the baby is dead. Check for yourself."

No telling how many young and inexperienced residents she has had to bring along in her career, I grimly thought as I quickly put on a mask, sterile gown and gloves from a bedside stand.

The nurse placed sterile lubricant on my index and middle fingers. I asked the patient, "Try to relax."

"Doctor," the nurse informed me, "she speaks no English."

"Do you speak Spanish?" I asked the nurse.

"Only a few words," she replied.

"Can you tell her to let her legs fall to the side?"

"No, but I can slowly press her knees down." As the nurse gradually pushed down her knees, the patient relaxed her legs.

As gently as I could, I inserted my two gloved fingers into her vagina, only to discover something I had never felt before: a soft, mushy fetal head. *The baby is dead*, I somberly realized.

I nodded my head to the nurse, and said quietly, "I agree with your assessment. There's no need to call the chief resident; nothing more can be done."

Before I could attempt to relate this to the patient, she screamed, and a hard contraction started. The baby's head began to bulge through the opening in the cervix. I told the patient one of the few words I knew in Spanish, *"Puje!,"* Spanish for "push."

With that, she bent her neck forward, and she grunted as she bore down, veins bulging out on the sides of her head.

In the next instant, I held my breath as a dead, macerated, full-term infant plopped out of the vagina into my waiting hands. It was horrible—I wanted to cry. I clamped the umbilical cord in two places, cut the cord in between and separated the dead baby from its mother.

I gazed down at the infant and pondered: *You never had a chance, did you?*

I asked the nurse, "Can you tell Senora Hernandez that her baby is dead?"

"I don't know the words."

Oh, my God, I thought to myself. "Can you find someone who can?"

"Yes," she said. "I'll be back in a moment.

The nurse rushed away, and I had no choice but to place the dead baby on the infant warmer standing beside me.

I then heard Maria question with the little English she knew, "Doc-tor? . . . Doc-tor?"

I removed my bloody gloves, threw them to the floor and

walked up next to her. Panic was written all over her sweaty face.

"Doc-tor?" she repeated, questioning.

I suddenly realized: *She never heard her baby cry.*

I looked at her dark, pleading eyes and glanced at the doorway for the translator. No one there. I had no choice but to say words I knew she would not understand, yet I hoped she would get the meaning. I pulled my mask from my face, shook my head from side-to-side and tersely said, "Your baby is dead."

First, a look of confusion crossed her face, and then abruptly she understood. She put her hands to her face and exclaimed, *"Doc-tor! No! Mi bebé! Muerto?"*

At that moment, the nurse, translator at her side, arrived and attempted to comfort her in a language she could understand.

I slowly walked away, forever changed. No longer would I look at labor and delivery with rose-colored glasses and always expect things to be fluffy and joyous, pink or blue. Some events in life, no matter how lofty one's perspective, are never all right—never. Every so often, we are reminded that the dark, dank, heavy shroud of death hangs over each and every one of us, even over helpless, innocent babies.

At that grim instant, I had no words in my vocabulary to help console Maria. I was gagged and mute in an empty moment that ached to be filled with conciliatory and comforting words. All I had to offer this unfortunate woman in her greatest time of need was silence.

So much for joyful, blessed events . . .

Chapter 15

THE BUCKING BRONCHO

No sane person relishes the idea of having a spinal tap. Also known as a lumbar puncture (LP), the procedure has engendered tales, mostly urban legends, that abound with horrible experiences some have had, such as paralysis, numbness down the legs, chronic back pain, headaches or, God forbid, death.

Most of these fears are completely unfounded, though a relatively common drawback is a post-LP headache. This unfortunate side effect is caused by a leak of the spinal fluid after the procedure and can occur in anywhere from five to forty percent of patients. If the headaches are particularly agonizing—and they can be—to obtain relief a blood patch can be done. For this procedure, twenty to thirty milliliters of blood are drawn from the patient and injected around the area where the LP was performed. This forms a clot and most of the time this simple intervention will stop the leak of spinal fluid and the patient's headache.

The reasons to carry out an LP are numerous, though the most common is for spinal anesthesia. Besides, an LP can help diagnose serious infections such as encephalitis, syphilis, and meningitis. LP can also pick up conditions such as subarachnoid hemorrhages—dangerous types of brain bleeds—some cancers of the brain or spinal cord, as well as inflammatory disorders such as Guillain-Barre syndrome or multiple sclerosis.

My initial experience with an LP came firsthand, when I had spinal anesthesia for knee surgery. Previously, I had torn the medial meniscus of my right knee while playing for the medical school flag football team, and, unfortunately, the injury resisted conservative treatment. Since I was a medical student, I had the honor and privilege of having my LP performed by the director of anesthesia at the University of Oklahoma Medical College, Doctor Stanley Deutsch. The LP itself was relatively painless and uncomplicated, but for several hours afterward I had the rather distressing problem of being unable to urinate, which was associated with the absence of feeling in my groin, lower abdomen and legs. With the healing power of time and the caring reassurance of the nursing staff, to my relief, all was ultimately well again.

I clearly recall the first time I performed an LP. I was a third year medical student on my pediatrics rotation at Children's Hospital in Oklahoma City, circa 1975. Now, in retrospect, I don't recall the reason for performing the LP, but I was pleased, though a bit nervous, when my resident asked me to do the procedure. As the patient was a slender, cooperative, twelve-year-old male child, the situation could not have been more ideal. A motto at teaching hospitals is, "See one, do one, teach one." I had carefully observed several LPs beforehand, and I was ready.

Under the resident's direct supervision, the child was laid on his left side, and, with the assistance of a nurse, his legs were flexed into his chest, while his head and neck were gently bent forward. Positioning is critical to the success of an LP, as the fetal position opens up the interspaces of the back, allowing easier access through the layers of tissue into the subarachnoid space, the location of the spinal fluid.

Initially wearing non-sterile gloves, I identified the point of entry for the LP and marked it by gently indenting the skin with a fingernail. These gloves were then replaced with sterile ones, and the skin was thoroughly cleaned with Betadine and isopropyl alcohol. After sterile paper drapes were applied, the area was numbed with local anesthesia, and I took a deep, calming breath before I inserted the spinal needle. Applying consistent, firm pressure and angling cephalad—toward the patient's head—I eventually felt a distinct pop, indicating that I had advanced the needle through the dura, the tough, outermost membrane that envelops the brain and spinal cord.

Much to my relief, when I removed the stylet of the needle, clear spinal fluid freely dripped into a collection tube. Once I had gathered the necessary amount, I replaced the stylet back into the needle and removed it from the child's lower back. I then placed a *Band-Aid* over the puncture site and, to my amazement and relief, the LP was successfully completed. I glanced up at my resident, who had been thoughtfully talking me through the procedure. Our eyes met, he nodded his head and smiled. I could not have felt better.

Through the course of my medical school training, I performed a number of LPs, and over the years to come, the total carried out swelled into the hundreds. I have always tried to "Zen" my way through each and every one—carefully evaluating every patient's particular anatomy—and, realizing how anxiety-provoking an LP can be, I talk to the patient before, during, and after the procedure. I use the smallest possible needle, as the evidence clearly demonstrates this decreases the incidence of the previously described post-LP headache. I have habitually brought a sense of urgency and caution with me into every LP that I have performed, and while I've not been able to complete all of them, it's not for lack of giving it my best.

Little did I know way back then, that in the twilight of my career, I'd be faced with a case that would be much more challenging, a situation that would demand every ounce of skill that I possessed, one that would make my initial LP seem like a walk in the park.

The symptom of confusion, or what we in emergency medicine call altered level of consciousness, is an extremely common
and oftentimes serious problem. This complaint is most prevalent
in the elderly and can be due to a number of different causes, a few
of the more common ones being low blood sugar, lack of oxygen,
overwhelming infection, a stroke or transient ischemic attack (TIA),
alcohol or drug intoxication, alcohol withdrawal and diabetic ketoacidosis. These possible diagnoses just scratch the surface of a very
long and complicated list.

One autumn morning in the emergency department, I pulled
a chart from the "To Be Seen" rack. The patient was a sixty-two-year-
old female, and the chief complaint read, "Altered level of consciousness." Vital signs on the chart revealed a pulse rate of 120, with normal blood pressure, respirations, temperature and oxygen saturation.

I went to the patient's room and found her nurse in attendance. "What's the story?" I asked.

"Sixty-two-year-old female just brought in by ambulance
from her home with a history of new onset confusion. She just
moved here from Montana, so she currently has no family doctor."

"When was she last known to be normal?" I asked, knowing
that while a stroke was unlikely in this age group, if the patient presents within four and a half hours after the onset of symptoms, he or
she might be a candidate for TPA, a clot busting medication recommended by the American Heart Association.

"The paramedic said she was well when she went to bed
around ten p.m. She was discovered in this condition at eight this
morning."

I asked, "What was her fingerstick blood glucose?"

"Unremarkable at one hundred-twenty."

"I see. Any family here yet?"

"No, but they're supposed to be coming in."

"Good. Is she on any medications?"

"The paramedic brought in a list. They include hydrocodone for chronic back pain, meds for hypertension and high cholesterol."

Overdose? I wondered.

"What about anticoagulants?" I questioned, thinking this could possibly be a head bleed.

"No, none," the nurse responded.

"Okay, let me examine her. Thanks for the information."

The nurse returned to other chores, and I went into the room to evaluate the patient. She was morbidly obese, combative, and both of her pupils were round and reactive to light. Her neck was supple, her heart and lungs were normal, and her abdomen was soft and non-tender. Neurologically, she was moaning incoherently, and she did not respond to questioning, but was moving both of her upper and lower extremities symmetrically.

Coming out of the room, I saw the patient's nurse sitting at her desk in front of a computer. "Let me know when her family arrives," I requested. "I'll post her orders soon. To collect the urine, would you please place a Foley catheter with a temperature probe?"

I walked to my desk and sat quietly for a moment. At that point, I had to confess this case completely baffled me.

Shortly afterward, her lab tests revealed that something serious was going on. Her white blood count was high at 33,000, normal being less than 11,000. Her urinalysis revealed a urinary tract infection, and her drug screen was positive for opiates—narcotics. The CAT scan of her head was normal, showing no evidence of stroke or hemorrhage, and her other tests were unremarkable.

Her husband arrived and confirmed the story told to me by the nurse, except for one small, but important detail, which was that she complained of an earache the night before. Realizing that a rare complication of a middle ear infection was meningitis, I began to question: *Could she have meningitis? But she had no fever, and her neck was freely moveable, not rigid.* Without those symptoms, that diagnosis seemed unlikely.

At that moment, though, the nurse walked up to me and said, "Remember the Foley you asked me to place with a temperature probe?"

"Yes."

"The temperature was initially normal. Now it's reading 102 degrees."

I paused for only a moment. I asked her nurse, "Please set her up for an LP."

After obtaining consent from her husband, I knew without a doubt that this would be one of the toughest LPs I had ever attempted. The first problem was her obesity. *Would the standard three-and-a-half-inch needle be long enough?* Second was the issue of her combativeness. She would have to be sedated, but her level of consciousness was already altered. I knew it was risky, but there was no other option, an LP had to be performed. The jeopardy I would put the patient in was necessary, as I was dealing with a matter of life and death. Making this diagnosis could not wait.

As four helpers huddled around the patient's bed in anticipation, I instructed the RN in attendance, "Please give her a milligram of Ativan IV."

While many different medications are available for sedation purposes, for this instance I chose Ativan, a benzodiazepine and a member of the Valium family of drugs. While effective, one of the known side effects of this medication is respiratory depression, in other words, it could potentially slow or stop breathing.

I began to set up the LP tray while the nursing staff maneuvered the patient to her left side. The nurses positioned her correctly, although she remained combative.

As they began to put her in a fetal position, she began to fight and kick, much to my dismay.

"Another milligram of Ativan, please," I asked.

After she was sedated and placed in position, I prepped the area of entry for the LP and applied sterile drapes. When I began to numb her, she once again began to struggle and lurch in the bed.

"One more milligram of Ativan," I requested, feeling a bit apprehensive about the patient's breathing, but her oxygen saturation remained normal, so I continued with the procedure.

Because of her obesity, the anatomical landmarks I needed to perform the LP were difficult to locate. After carefully pausing, checking and rechecking, I placed the needle through the skin. I patiently advanced it, but well before I had reached the subarachnoid space, I met bony resistance.

Damn! I thought to myself.

I withdrew the needle and took a slightly different angle, holding my breath.

Once again I met a bony impediment, one that blocked the progress of the needle. *The angle of entry must not be correct,* I thought. Once again, I again pulled it out.

The patient again began to pitch back and forth like a bucking bronco. The nursing staff intensified their grip on her.

Perspiration began to bead up on my forehead. I was generous in the amount of Lidocaine I had used for local anesthesia, so I was certain she was numb and the punctures were not the cause of her agitation. I ordered, "Another milligram of Ativan, please. And," I said to my helpers as I forced a smile, "You're all doing a great job. Hang in there."

It's now or never, I thought to myself. Once again the patient was calmed, so I re-inserted the needle and took a more acute angle towards her head. No resistance occurred this time, though I almost used the full length of the needle before I felt the hoped for pop that indicated I had entered the subarachnoid space. When I withdrew the stylet from the spinal needle, grossly purulent fluid—pus—flowed into the collection tube.

Bacterial meningitis, I concluded with certainty.

Unfortunately, she once again began to thrash uncontrollably. The nursing staff courageously held on for dear life as I once again ordered, "One more milligram of Ativan." I glanced up at the monitor that demonstrated the oxygen saturation level—still normal.

This time the Ativan didn't help. The patient's combativeness continued, even though a needle protruded from her back, so I had to abort the LP. I had obtained only a small sample of spinal fluid, but I knew I had enough to make a diagnosis.

I pulled out the needle, yet the patient continued to struggle. I dared not give her any more sedation, for, as Hippocrates so wisely said, "Primum non nocere," which translated, means, "First, do no harm." Giving her further meds had the potential to stop her breathing and wasn't worth the risk. We could keep her from hurting herself by applying soft restraints.

The patient was then given steroids and high doses of antibiotics. In spite of our efforts, the clinical outlook was grim, and I felt the risk of death was very high.

The patient was admitted to ICU with a diagnosis of Streptococcal meningitis, and she remained comatose for several days. Then, much to my delight, she regained consciousness and eventually recovered. Due to her combativeness at the time she was under my care, I was unable to examine her ears, but I later discovered she indeed had a right ear infection—an otitis media—which had led to a rip-roaring case of bacterial meningitis.

Emergency physicians have cases during their careers that are especially challenging, ones that test them to the maximum. This specific one certainly was a trial for me, but more than that, never in my wildest dreams would I have ever guessed that someday, like a rodeo cowboy, I would have to find a way to tame a bucking bronco. Yet, I somehow did, and I felt much like I did when I completed that first LP all those years ago.

As we in Oklahoma might say:
Yee-haw!

Chapter 16

LAUGHTER IS THE BEST MEDICINE

One of my favorite stories concerns the amazing Norman Cousins, a 20th century optimist who was known for his love of life and kindness to others. He was an author, a journalist and an advocate of nuclear disarmament and world peace. He was also an adjunct professor at UCLA, where he conducted studies on the biochemistry of human emotions, which he believed were critical to a person's success in fighting disease.

Late in life, Cousins was diagnosed with ankylosing spondylitis, a painful chronic inflammatory disease that primarily affects the sacroiliac joints, the hips, and the spine. He was told by his physician that he was unlikely to survive this illness, and he should get his affairs in order.

Rather than giving up and going to his bed to die, Cousins fired his doctor, found a physician who would work with him and his ideas, and developed his own personal healing program. He began to take high doses of intravenous Vitamin C in combination with uproarious laughter brought on by viewing various comic films and videos of the television series, *Candid Camera*. He once remarked, "I made the joyous discovery that ten minutes of genuine belly laughter had an anesthetic effect and would give me at least two hours of pain-free sleep. When the pain-killing effect of the laughter wore off, we would switch on the motion picture projector again and not infrequently, it would lead to another pain-free interval."

Cousins eventually went into remission and chronicled his story in the book, *Anatomy of an Illness*. While, in retrospect, it has been speculated that Cousins may have actually had post-streptococcal reactive arthritis, the relevance of his narrative, when he fought tooth and nail against seemingly impossible odds, remains unchanged. In 1990, Norman Cousins died, and I would say that he was more than just an interesting man; he was someone who practiced what he preached, a true rarity in this day and age.

With this background in mind, is it any wonder, given the stress health care providers are subjected to, that laughter is often used to maintain their sanity? Nowadays, we know that laughter releases endorphins, natural mood-elevating compounds, which can be of great benefit when people are under pressure. Stories abound in the emergency department of the gags we subjected each other to in order to keep things from getting too heavy. I fondly recall that on night shifts, one of the nurses found a radio station that frequently played a song in which chickens clucked to the tune of Glenn Miller's "In the Mood." Anytime it came on the radio, the nurse at the desk would turn the volume up and we would shake and grind like we were at a rock concert. In retrospect, it seems a bit off-the-wall that we enjoyed listening to it so much, but the music made us smile, and this comic pause provided some relief from our stress. I still recall one night when the emergency department had been particularly busy. Around five a.m., exhausted, I limped back to the sleep room to catch a few winks. I had just fallen fast asleep and was dreaming when I heard the phone ring.

I thought: *Already, another patient?*

I somehow aroused and picked up the phone. "Hello?"

All I heard, besides the pealing laughter of the nursing staff in the background, was a bunch of chickens bock bock bocking "In the Mood." I felt like murdering the nurses I worked with, and yet, I softly chuckled before I hung up the phone.

I grin as I think about all of the practical jokes we played on each other. Anything was fair game—anything. A certain incident still sticks out in my mind. One of the younger physicians in our group, Mike, had just discovered he had passed his emergency medicine boards, and several hours before his shift was to begin, a surprise congratulatory gift for him arrived at the emergency department from his proud wife, Kelly. The delivery was from Sweete Memories, a specialty bakery located in the aristocratic, highbrow section of town. The gift basket was of the highest quality and was packed with all sorts of scrumptious delicacies which sat on a crisp, manicured bed of green crepe. The bakery items were no doubt prepared by a top French dessert chef and made with the finest ingredients.

Naturally, the nurses and I thought that this gift of the wealthy class was prime fodder for a laugh, so we carefully unwrapped it, removed the gourmet delights packed inside and replaced them with hospital snacks. For any who have ever been around a hospital emergency department, you can only imagine how bad this was: bunches of soggy grapes that looked like raisins, rotten oranges with blue, moldy spots on them, bananas that were mostly black, and individually wrapped saltine and graham crackers. Much like typical outdated hospital food, this was the worst of the worst.

Later, when Mike arrived for his shift, I announced, "Hey Mike, looks like you've got something here from Sweete Memories. Someone must love you an awful lot!"

He first read the note from his wife, though his eyes widened ever so slightly as he inspected the contents of the basket. Meanwhile, the nurses and I were doing all we could to keep up a serious front.

Finally, he picked up the phone and punched out some numbers. He said, "Kelly, you won't believe what's in this basket from Sweete Memories. I can't imagine . . ."

At that point we all burst into laughter and Mike knew he'd been had. We then pulled out all the items we had taken from the basket and presented them to him. I thought it took a lot of will power for us not to sample them beforehand.

Of course, we would *never* stoop that low.

Probably the most common humorous tales involve critters, especially scary ones. Often patients who'd suffered some kind of bite would bring the nasty varmints that had bitten them to the emergency department for identification, just to make sure they weren't going to die a miserable, agonizing paralytic death from something poisonous. While I've looked at many mashed spiders, scorpions, ticks, centipedes, mice, and rats, my favorite ones were the snakes. Identifying poisonous vs. nonpoisonous varieties is not difficult, and I might venture to guess that over 95% of snakes brought in for me to inspect were non-venomous, and they could bite someone over a hundred times, and no harm would come to the patient, except, of course, psychologically. Once the patients were reassured, the snake was invariably left behind, which led to all sorts of trickery and pranks.

I vividly recall a large, six-foot-long black snake that was brought with a patient who had been bitten. The snake had been quickly crushed with a shovel and was barely identifiable, but it was clearly dead—dead as a car battery in wintertime Antarctica.

For some reason, the favorite transport for snakes brought in from home was the brown paper grocery sack, and this situation was no different. As I stood there, snake-containing bag in hand, nurse after nurse warily peeked over the side of the sack, looked at the contents within, and quickly moved away. To this day, I'm not certain why people want to see things that scare the bejeebies out of them, such as spine-tingling horror movies.

I waited for my chance, and at last I saw my victim, a woman from housekeeping, who for some reason just had to see the snake. She was obviously scared, and she warily crept up to the sack, trembling in fear. As she stuck her head over the side to take a quick peek, I shook the sack, causing the dead snake to catapult out of the top of the bag.

I yelled, "Look out! It's still alive!"

She jumped back, screamed a blood-curdling scream, and howled as she dashed as quickly as she could out of the emergency department, arms flailing above her head. All present roared with laughter, tears rolling down our faces.

After that incident, I never saw her again in the emergency department. It wasn't hard to understand why.

Then, I realized that, in spite of the repeated blows from a garden tool, this was the best specimen of a snake I had seen in some time, and what a shame it would be if I scared only one person with it. This valuable resource had to be utilized to its fullest potential. I thought and thought, and at last my calculating mind came up with the obvious answer. Looking back now, I shudder at what I decided to do. *What was I thinking?*

But at that moment, it made sense. I was certain who my next prey would be: Pam, the nurse manager.

Surely, she could handle a joke . . . right?

I was in the middle of a night shift, and I had discharged the last remaining patient at six a.m. When I confirmed no one was watching, I surreptitiously crept into Pam's unlocked office, carrying with me the bag containing the snake. I looked around for the ideal location to deposit the serpent for maximal effect, and soon enough, I found it—in her desk. I opened the top drawer, and I discovered a nice empty niche just perfect for a dead reptile. I coiled it up and jammed it inside, hoping that I had not been seen by anyone. I could hardly wait until she came in to work in the morning.

Daytime arrived, and imagine my disappointment when she came and went out of her office through the morning and nothing happened. All of my patients had been discharged, and I'm sure she was beginning to wonder why I was still hanging around. At long last, I received the ultimate reward. She returned to her office, and moments later she danced out, arms gyrating and screaming at the top of her lungs.

When she finally returned to her office with reinforcements at hand, she happily realized the snake was dead and was gradually able to calm herself. The entire emergency department, though, was in stitches—pun intended. Pam glanced over at me as I was struggling to maintain my composure, and immediately she knew the truth of the matter. Since we were friends, I speculated: *Hopefully, she wouldn't be too upset with me?*

While this little prank seemed like the right thing to do at the time, even hilarious in my way of thinking, I didn't realize that I had made a stupendous mistake in judgment. The nurses, who stuck together like sorority sisters, would find a way to get even with the one—me—who had frightened their leader out of her mind. No doubt they felt the need to take up for Pam and also the housekeeper, who was likely, thanks to me, now at a mental institution under heavy sedation, taking anti-psychotic drugs and having nightmares and hallucinations about snakes.

Payback was in store.

But the nurses would plan their retribution carefully. It would be delivered at some carefully determined time in the future when I least expected it, after I'd forgotten all about the snake in the desk incident.

Several months later, I was working in the emergency department, and it had been a tough night. Around four a.m. I had at last cleared the place out, and I was looking forward to getting some shuteye. I was distracted and tired, and somehow I missed the little happy smirks that were passing back and forth between the nurses. I stumbled toward the sleep room and keyed in the code to the door. Entering, I pulled down the bedcovers, flipped off the light switch and crawled in.

The minute my feet reached the foot of the bed, I knew something was terribly wrong. I felt something cold and slimy. I gasped and let out a high-pitched scream. I leapt from the bed and after regaining my senses, cautiously pulled the covers all the way down. I jumped back as I saw a snake curled up at the foot of the bed. But as I looked closer, I noticed it wasn't moving. Gathering my courage, I moved a little nearer and discovered that my assailant was actually just a large rubber replica of a snake, one that was coated with a thick layer of K-Y Jelly.

After relief flooded my being, I couldn't help but smile. I picked up the phone to let the nurses know that they had successfully scared the holy Hell out of me. I heard peals of unbridled laughter, and I'm sure the housekeeper would have approved of my punishment.

For at least a short while, though, as with those earlier months when I first scared my ex-friend, Pam, the nurse manager, the pain we had to deal with in our day-to-day jobs had temporarily vaporized. Return it would, but for now, the strain and worries of the emergency department were forgotten in the midst of a great belly laugh.

Norman Cousins was right.

Laughter *is* the best medicine.

Chapter 17

SYNCOPE

P robably one of the most embarrassing and humiliating experiences that can happen to a medical student, or any health care provider for that matter, is to have a syncopal episode, or, in laymen's terms, a fainting spell.

After a few years of being constantly presented in their training with varied, challenging encounters, medical students gradually become inured—hardened—to distressing situations. But that quality doesn't come immediately. Such requires multiple exposures to shocking, unsettling incidents before the students become Teflon men or women, much like President Ronald Reagan to whom nothing would stick.

The only time I came close to taking a dive was when, as described in *Oklahoma Is Where I Live,* I went to labor and delivery, hoping to observe the delivery of a baby. Arriving too late, I had barely walked into the room, when the new mother bore down, screamed and pushed out her placenta. I was nearly done in by the combination of the sharp, acrid smell of blood and the peculiar sloshing sound made by the placenta as it plopped into a stainless-steel basin.

But my experience was the rule, not the exception. Most medical students had at least one encounter with near-syncope or syncope during their training. I recall how one of my colleagues was observing a hernia surgery when he passed out. All would have been forgiven if he had simply buckled and fallen straight down or backwards, but to the surgeon's chagrin, he unfortunately toppled face forward, right on top of the patient, sterile drapes flying everywhere. I might guess the surgeon blew a gasket when his pristine surgical field—this was in the days prior to laparoscopy—was contaminated when the student drooled and maybe even vomited right into the abdominal cavity. How would the surgeon explain the likely post-operative infection to his patient?

Syncope can occur anytime, anyplace, and in medical students the most common cause is vasovagal. In this situation, certain sensory triggers, such as the sight of blood, a strong odor or extreme stress, stimulate the vagus nerve. This causes the heart rate and the blood pressure to abruptly drop, which in seconds leads to a decrease in the flow of blood to the brain, causing the unlucky one to lose consciousness.

As a student, one learns to look for the telltale signs that a colleague is about to go to ground. I'll never forget the time when I was with a group of my fellow medical students in the ICU, observing a physician performing an emergency "cut down" procedure in hope of finding a vein for IV placement. He injected the area with a local anesthetic, and then he made an incision and began dissecting through the subcutaneous tissue in search of a suitable vein.

All seemed to be going well, at least until I glanced over at one of my fellow students, Ted, who was my buddy when we attended Oklahoma State University. Ted had a pale complexion to go along with his flaming red hair, but at that moment the color of his skin was akin to that of Frosty the Snowman. Not only that, but also Ted was sweaty, tottering, and looked like he was about to acquaint his face with the grey tiled, hospital floor.

It's worth mentioning that those who are about to faint nearly always deny there is a problem. Ted was no exception to this inviolate rule, so a lot of convincing was required to get him to sit down in an adjacent chair and put his head down between his legs. He finally did, and eventually Ted pinked up and looked once again like he belonged to the land of the living.

Another commonality to episodes of syncope in the hospital setting is that each and every one will be remembered in a humorous manner by those in attendance. As a result, every so often, when doctors and nurses catch a rare slow moment, we will sit and tell stories of those who have passed out over the years.

A favorite fodder for conversation at my hospital concerned one of the scribes in the emergency department who passed out while observing a lumbar puncture. Until the day she left our hospital to attend medical school, we kidded her mercilessly about the need to acquire a football helmet to protect her head the next time she bit the dust.

While all of the episodes of syncope are memorable to some degree, over all my years, not one is as indelibly etched in my memory as the fainting incident that occurred to a colleague of mine in the first year of medical school.

When I was at the University of Oklahoma Medical School, our class was divided into small groups, also called modules, where we could be instructed in more intimate settings about subjects not amenable to larger gatherings. Sixteen were in our module, and, with time, a deep, lasting camaraderie developed among us. We studied, laughed, cried, and suffered together, all unified by the common goal of trying to find a way to get through the travails of medical school. Even though there were sixteen in our group, we were much like The Three Musketeers, all for one, and one for all.

One day in the middle of our second semester, our module instructor announced that we were going to learn how to run the test to determine what our respective blood types were. To get the specimens for this undertaking, we had to obtain blood samples from each other.

Since this was the first time for most of us to draw blood, a number of us were a bit jittery. For me, though, I looked forward to learning this new skill, one I knew I would have to master in my third year of medical school. Besides, the person sitting next to me—my assigned phlebotomist—was the cool-as-a-cucumber, unflappable Liz. Nervousness was not part of her emotional repertoire, and she approached situations she was confronted with in an analytical, level-headed way. No one in my medical school class could be trusted more than she was to take my blood, and that's saying something. In a way, she reminded me of Mr. Spock on Star Trek, except that I don't ever recall Liz holding her fingers in the Vulcan salute and telling me to "Live long and prosper."

There were eight of us in our half of the module, and across the room sat my friends, John and Max. Both were tall and slender, though John had brown hair and Max's was black. I glanced over at them while our instructor was readying the materials for this grand scientific endeavor, and it appeared to me that they both looked more-than-a-little nervous.

I wondered: *Why are they worried? The worst that can happen is that the person drawing the blood might miss, and a repeat attempt might be necessary*—just shows how much I knew. Once the laboratory supplies were distributed, Liz and I determined that she would draw my blood first. She readied the collection tubes, and then placed a rubber tourniquet around my upper arm.

"Open and close your fist," she requested. With that, the veins in my arm began to enlarge, and she calmly attached a needle to the syringe, removed the protective cap and steadily inserted it into my vein. She then effortlessly aspirated my blood into the syringe.

No sweat, I thought.

Since things were going well, I took the opportunity to glance over at John and Max, and I discovered an entirely different situation. John was drawing blood from Max, and a tourniquet had been placed just above Max's elbow. John's eyes were bulging as he approached Max with syringe in hand, violently shaking side-to-side as he neared Max's arm. While John looked horrified, Max looked even worse. On his face was a look of sheer panic. His eyes were opened even wider than John's, and he was pale and sweaty. Even though his right arm was in position to have his blood drawn, the rest of his body was pulled back, like he was trying to escape. Max's mouth was open wide, and he looked as if he was about to scream.

"I'm all done," Liz proclaimed, bringing my attention back. She popped the tourniquet loose and pulled the needle from my arm. She had just applied a *Band-Aid* when I heard a loud *thump*.

A collective gasp went up from those in the module, and I quickly looked over and discovered that Max had passed out, sliding out of his chair and landing back-first on the unyielding, linoleum floor. The tourniquet was still in place on his arm, and he said not a word—he was out cold. John appeared to be in a state of shock, but at least he had taken a moment to remove the tourniquet. I couldn't see blood anywhere; apparently the vein was never punctured, which came as no big surprise.

Liz and I stood up in concern, as did the rest of our module-mates, and several of us edged toward them. But then, Max's wife, Loretta, with her slender build, long dark hair and pale complexion, unexpectedly strolled into the module. She put her hands to her face, inhaled deeply as she saw her husband lying motionless on the floor and loudly screamed, "Oh Max!"

As an RN nursing student, Loretta was wearing her navy blue and white school uniform. She quickly assumed control of the situation, rushed over to Max, sat on the floor, and cradled his head in her lap. With the tenderness of Florence Nightingale and the skill of

Clara Barton, Loretta stroked his head with her thumbs as he slowly came around.

"Maxey, baby, are you okay? Maxey, honey, I'm right here," she tenderly murmured. Max gradually became more alert, and when Liz and I realized that Max was okay, we sighed and sat back down in our chairs.

As Loretta continued her consolations to her dear, stricken husband, the circumstances somehow morphed from serious to humorous. Liz and I both found ourselves doing all we could to keep from laughing.

"Oh Max, honey, you're going to be okay." Loretta said as she moved her massaging fingers from his forehead down to his temples. "I love you, baby," she added.

Finally, I couldn't take it anymore, and I began to snort, trying ever-so-hard to keep from guffawing. Soon, the entire module started to snicker, and every so often, someone burst out in a peal of laughter.

Max, now perfectly alert, though still lying on the floor, was embarrassed beyond words. He glanced around the room, and then he muttered to Loretta in a gravelly voice, "Leave me alone."

After hearing his words and seeing the stunned look on Loretta's face, everyone in the module started heehawing and rolling on the floor laughing, and any semblance of control completely disappeared. Our module instructor, who first looked concerned by the incident, tried to assume a serious air, but he was betrayed by a slight twinkle in his eyes.

I wiped the tears of laughter from my face, looked over at Liz and asked, "Are you ready for me to draw your blood?"

"Sure," she answered as she dabbed her eyes with a tissue. "Just give me a few moments to regain my composure."

As I thought about it, not only was I glad to be aware that Liz was not just another Mr. Spock as I had imagined, I was also ecstatic beyond words to know that I had just experienced an event that would make me laugh for the rest of my life.

Even now, forty-four years later, as I compose this story, I find myself chuckling. I will never forget this tale, and I have a feeling that Max won't either.

Chapter 18

LAWSUITS

As I evaluate my misdiagnoses in emergency medicine, several distinct categories become apparent. The first grouping is typified by the statements:
"You've got to be kidding! They had *what*?"

This is the dreaded red herring, the case that is so odd and so unbelievable, that even Star Trek's Bones, armed with his beeping tricorder, would have missed the diagnosis. I've had a number of these types of situations over the years, and they always leave me scratching my head and wondering what I could have done differently. I want to say I learned from these experiences, but the truth is that most of these cases were so rare and off-the-wall, I'll likely never see any of them again as long as I walk the halls of the emergency department.

In the second type, the patient exhibits symptoms early, but the real diagnosis is initially not apparent. I recall such an instance from many years ago, when a five-year-old child was brought in after being feverish for several hours. He had no vomiting, no diarrhea and had a mild cough. On examination, the child appeared vigorous and active, what we in emergency medicine would describe as nontoxic. The only physical finding I detected was dull, red eardrums, and so I confidently sent him home with a prescription for the antibiotic amoxicillin.

Later that night, I was informed by one of the nurses, "Doctor Conrad, you won't believe it, but that child that you saw earlier is back."

"What?" I exclaimed in disbelief. "What seems to be the problem?"

"The mother says he's getting worse, and he's not acting right."

"Bring him back right now," I demanded.

The minute I looked at him, I knew something was terribly wrong. He was poorly responsive, lethargic, and he looked—dare I say it—toxic, in other words, like a child who might have sepsis, a toxic condition resulting from the spread of pathogenic bacteria. The nursing staff and I went to work on him immediately, blood was drawn, urine was collected, and IV antibiotics were quickly given. When I performed the spinal tap, the usually clear-as-water spinal fluid was cloudy—like milk—certainly bacterial meningitis.

The specimen was rushed to the lab, and microscopic analysis revealed gram negative organisms typical for Haemophilus, a type of infection prevented in more recent times with a simple Hib vaccination. The child was promptly taken by ambulance to a nearby facility that specialized in pediatric care, and he did well, much to my relief.

This case is a prime example why most emergency physicians live in a land of neurosis and paranoia, with a near-constant low level of anxiety that every patient will find a way to go sour. That's at least part of the reason why follow up on a timely basis is always recommended to our patients. We have a saying in emergency medicine: If it seems too easy, it probably is.

The third category of misdiagnosis is one that has happened

to every clinician, even if only on the rarest of occasions. This is when, in retrospect, the diagnosis is obvious, and the doctor wonders: *How did I miss it?*

How does an emergency physician, or for that matter, any health care provider, make this sort of mistake? While there are numerous possibilities, one of the more common reasons occurs when one's mind becomes sidetracked and the diagnostic clues gathered while taking a history and performing a physical mislead the doctor down an alternative pathway. When the caregiver focuses on that spurious choice, it's difficult to turn back. Physicians would be helped if the emergency department had a quiet and soothing environment, with the calming, serene music of Mozart softly playing in the background, along with plenty of time to painstakingly scrutinize each and every case.

But such is never the situation. Besides being frequently swarmed over with many critically-ill patients, one has to deal with the egos and idiosyncrasies of fellow physicians, the demands of the nursing staff, worried family members, computerized charting systems, and the inherent issues in dealing with other ancillary hospital personnel who may not be having the best day of their lives.

With no intention to make excuses, it's hard to imagine a job tougher than that of the emergency department physician. Most patients are totally new to them, except for those who come to the emergency department on a regular basis and have their own unique set of problems. The doctor has to condense years of sometimes complex, complicated histories from a short interview and examination. After a series of diagnostic studies are completed, the emergency physician is expected to correctly figure out the diagnosis, even in the midst of all the mayhem. The critical on-the-spot decisions required can make the difference between life, death, or disablement for the patient.

In our litigious society, the potential consequence of missing a diagnosis is a lawsuit, and there's nothing a doctor despises more than being taken to court for alleged malpractice. When a physician goes through litigation, and nearly everyone will at some time in his or her career, it's akin to someone taking a dull knife, cutting open the physician's abdomen with a zigzag incision—without anesthesia— and watching as their steaming guts spill out for the world to see.

It's that bad.

Anytime someone the physician has provided care for has an unexpected bad outcome, he hurts—there's no other way around it. Every doctor demands perfection of himself, and being less than one hundred percent accurate is simply unacceptable. While such a fault-less performance is not humanly possible, it is expected by not only the physician, but also by everyone else involved—the patient, the family, and especially the hospital administration.

How does the physician discover he is being sued? Some-times, a bad result gives one a clue, and on occasion the grapevine will give a hint, but more often than not, the health care provider is completely blindsided.

The scenario could go like this; the doctor strolls out to his mailbox one day, whistling a happy tune, thinking about the upcom-ing, long-delayed vacation with his wife and children. Coincidental-ly, he runs into his mailperson, who presents him with a thick, cer-tified letter from a law firm. As the physician signs for it, his heart sinks to the floor and he prays to God that it's only a request for med-ical records.

When he opens the envelope and learns that he is being sued, he goes inside his home and plops down in the closest chair, takes deep breaths and tries to get a grip on himself. If he happens to have a prescription for Xanax on hand, he takes several tablets in hope of preventing an episode of hyperventilation. Not only is his day ruined, but also his vacation, if he even goes, and all the upcoming weeks, months or years until the case is settled, one way or another.

This initial time of discovery is followed by meeting with

one's lawyer, and later comes the much-dreaded deposition interview, where a stern, humorless, beady-eyed plaintiff's attorney in a
three-piece suit, or, if a woman, a dark business suit, asks all sorts
of probing and sometimes irrelevant questions, hoping to catch the
doctor saying something awry or making an admission that can be
teased and ripped apart.

While this is purported to be a process to gain information
about the case, it's actually much more than that. Depending upon
the skill level of the opposing lawyer, the strengths and weaknesses of
the case are probed mercilessly, and any mistake uttered during the
deposition will be sure to reappear in court. The deposition grilling
can take hours, and when finished the doctor feels like a wet noodle,
limp, spineless and inert, a mere shell of his former self.

Assuming the case is not settled or dropped, and thankfully most are, finally comes the day of court, a time feared from the
very moment that certified letter was received. First, the selection
of the jury occurs, followed by the attorneys' opening statements.
A series of witnesses then make their appearance, some who profess
that the defendant is the worst doctor in the known Universe, and
they wouldn't trust him to treat their pet cockatiel, while others—
the ones on the physician's side—put him on a par with the great
Hippocrates.

Then arrives the moment he has been nervous about from
the very beginning: the examination on the witness stand. After answering in the affirmative the initial question, "Do you swear to tell
the truth, the whole truth, and nothing but the truth, so help you
God?", the interrogation begins. The only items missing from this
joyous experience are a hot overhead lamp, a bullwhip, and medieval
instruments of torture left over from the Inquisition.

Most plaintiff attorneys are good with words, and they ex-
ploit every trick in the book in an effort to make the doctor stumble.
The physician has been tutored in advance to measure every state-
ment carefully, and as in the deposition, observes with focused intent

how the attorney puts things. The courtroom is the playing field, the "home court" of the lawyer, territory foreign to most doctors, and the only thought that gives the physician comfort is that no lawyer, no matter how bright he or she is, knows more about medicine than he does.

I am reminded of a time I was subpoenaed to court to testify as an expert witness in a sexual assault case. As I sat there on the stand, the defense attorney queried me with the most stupid question I have ever been asked, anytime, anywhere.

He cleared his throat, looked me in the eyes and asked, "Doctor Conrad, do women produce sperm?"

I looked at him, puzzled and caught a bit off guard by the oddness and ridiculousness of the question, and I answered, "Sir, that would be a most unusual case."

The lawyer's face reddened as a series of chuckles and overt laughter went up from those sitting in the courtroom. I was quite pleased with my clever and witty response until it gradually dawned on me that I had made a bonehead mistake. The inquisitor's mood quickly turned from embarrassment to one of anger and hostility, and he subsequently lit into me with a fervor and relish that would have made Perry Mason proud.

Thirty minutes of Hell later, I humbly walked off the stand, shaking my head, tail between my legs, fully aware of the cost of trying to be a comedian in the courtroom.

After being battered by the plaintiff's lawyer like a ship caught in a typhoon at sea, what comes next is gentle, patient questioning by the doctor's own attorney, who in a soothing voice, tries to patch up the holes in the testimony, and give the physician the opportunity to redeem himself.

This temporary respite, an oasis of comfort, is then followed by a cross examination and a revisit into depths worthy of Dante's

Inferno. After a flood of perspiration and eventual exhaustion, the doctor's time on the stand ends, and he lets loose a deep sigh of relief. He stands from his chair and staggers a bit as he approaches the seat next to his attorney. While the depositions made him feel emotionally buffeted and weak, his time on the witness stand made him feel physically ill.

Finally, the attorneys for both sides give their closing statements, waxing eloquently in an attempt to sway the jury to their way of thinking. The jury is then dismissed to deliberate the case, and all the physician has to do now is to wait for their decision.

While there is an aura of anticipation about the verdict, and the doctor prays with all his heart that the jury will find in his favor, the damage has been done, win or lose. He is shattered on all levels, and he will never be the same person he once was. The wounds sustained through this process, over time, will become tender scars, never completely healing.

Unfortunately, his outlook on patients has probably been changed forever. Now the physician sees them not only as sick people seeking his help, but also as potential litigants who could strike out at him, in spite of his best efforts. As a matter of self-preservation, the doctor has a tendency to become wary and skeptical.

The wounded healer can be a powerful asset in understanding patients and their illnesses, but that's certainly not the case with lawsuits. While I agree that patients should be compensated when they have been injured by a negligent physician who practices below a certain standard of care, I believe the process should be one that educates rather than damns, understands rather than shames, one that recognizes imperfections are part of our nature.

The Dalai Lama once said, "My religion is kindness." There's nothing about our current medico-legal system that is kind, either to physicians or to their injured patients, who oftentimes have to wait many years to receive reparation from the damages they have sustained, and, once the case is finalized, have to pay up to 40% of the settlement amount to their attorney.

Change is in order, for the good of everyone involved.

Chapter 19

NOSOPHOBIA

A common phobia in our modern-day society is nosophobia, an irrational fear of contracting a disease. The origin of the word comes from Greek, *nosos* meaning 'disease,' and *phobos*, 'fear.'

As far as the general public is concerned, a frequent cause of nosophobia is excessive media exposure to varied illnesses. One subset of nosophobia is called cyberchondria, when people compulsively spend an inordinate amount of time specifically on the Internet, learning about frightening diseases, eventually bringing about states of disabling anxiety.

In my practice in emergency medicine, this problem crops up far more often than it used to, and dealing with a nosophobic patient can be not only frustrating, but can also be an enormous time drain. A typical conversation might go something like this:

I explain, "Mrs. Peabody, I've looked carefully at your laboratory evaluation and x-ray studies, and I'm fairly certain your abdominal pain is caused by an intestinal virus."

"But Doctor," she says with a look of panic on her face, "I've done an Internet search on my computer, and I have discovered a number of other possible causes. How can you be sure it's not appendicitis?"

"Appendicitis would have probably shown up on your CAT scan. Besides, your history and physical exam don't fit that diagnosis."

Mrs. Peabody looks as if she's about to cry. "But I saw some Internet websites that say my symptoms are identical to those caused by parasitic cecitis."

I fight back the urge to roll my eyes. "Anything is possible," I answer, trying not to sound condescending, "but that problem is quite rare. We have collected stool specimens for bacteria, ova and parasites. In the next three days, the results should be back, and we'll know for sure. I think . . ."

Mrs. Peabody interrupts and barely sobs out, "And I also read . . . that I could have widespread, *terminal* ovarian . . . cancer. There was a woman in Lithuania who had unexplained abdominal pain— just like mine—and by the time they found out she had . . . ovarian cancer, it was too late."

I feel exasperation beginning to grow. "Again, that would have most likely shown up on your CAT scan. Trust me; you don't have any kind of cancer."

She pulls out a wad of tissue from her purse, looks down at the floor and grumbles, "Whatever you say, Doctor. I'll check with my physician tomorrow and see if she agrees with you." She blows her nose, stuffs the tissue back in her purse, puts her nose up in the air and angrily rushes out of the emergency department.

Nosophobia also appears to be common among researchers and students who spend a large part of their time reading about certain illnesses. This has been called "medical students' disease," and part of the cause can be due to repeated contact with those who have different illnesses. Ordinary logic supplies the reason why. As an

example, a medical student has been seeing a patient with tuberculosis in the clinic, which has already been treated, and is not contagious. Like any good student, he reads all he can about the disease,
known in ancient times as consumption, and discovers symptoms of
this deadly scourge include a cough, chills, night sweats, weight loss,
fatigue, and/or fever. While the medical student knows intellectually that the patient cannot transmit his disease to him, he begins
thinking: *I've been losing weight lately, and I'm feeling pretty tired.
Besides, over the past few days, I've developed a cough and a bit of a
temperature.* For some reason, he somehow forgets that every medical student is fatigued and losing weight because of overwork and
stress. Besides, in his hospital work, he is constantly exposed to every
virus in the known universe, and to manifest a cough and fever on
occasion would generally be expected.

But these facts don't matter to him. After no small amount
of over-thinking and anxiety, he becomes convinced that he has a
raging case of tuberculosis, which leads him to journey to the health
department for a skin test, which, of course, turns out to be negative.
He breathes a sigh of relief, until he discovers that the next patient
he is assigned to care for was treated some months earlier for second-
ary syphilis, which was discovered after the patient presented with an
unusual rash. The medical student's mind begins to churn: *Didn't I
have an unexplained, odd rash last week?*

And so it goes . . .

One minor manifestation of nosophobia can occur when patients come to their clinician with scabies, which is a contagious skin
infestation caused by a microscopic mite, *Sarcoptes scabiei.* Whenever
faced with this problem, even though the nursing staff and I are careful to put on gloves and utilize barrier protection—such as protective gowns— invariably we find ourselves itching all over afterward,
thinking we have contracted the disease, though this is almost never
the case.

Another common example of nosophobia is excessive cleanliness. For some, the fear of contracting a life-threatening disease can be temporarily alleviated by keeping those dreaded germs under control, cleaning everything in sight with antiseptics. I recall in the olden days how the nursing staff literally bathed their work areas with isopropyl alcohol at the start of and during their shifts, and how some of my physician colleagues would periodically do the same treatment on their stethoscopes. I found great humor as I watched them go through their cleaning rituals, but now, oddly enough, after years of exposure to potentially infective blood, saliva, urine, and feces, I frequently find myself doing the very same thing.

If I ever doubted that I have some degree of nosophobia, all I have to do is to think back to an experience I had some time ago, one that makes me smile as I recall it.

Living in the middle of the boondocks east of Guthrie, Oklahoma, was a wonderful experience. Granted, the drive to work in the Oklahoma City area was long and hard to deal with on a day-to-day basis, but the quietness of the rural countryside and the overall advantages of living without the urban hustle and bustle made the lengthy travel well worthwhile.

Like any rural setting, though, the varmints in the area were numerous, plentiful, and hungry. Possums, raccoons, snakes, armadillos, squirrels, skunks, mice, and rats lived there in abundance, fiercely competing with each other for any morsels of food that might come their way. For a while, I had a problem with an infestation of mice and rats in my garage. While waiting for poison to eradicate the little pests—I know, I don't like killing anything, but what was I supposed to do?—I temporarily relocated the dog food container to the front porch. I had hoped that other varmints would make it a point not to wander too close to the home of dangerous humans, especially since my dogs were very protective of their food. Unfortunately, the dogs, after a few brief sorties to the food bowl, didn't care enough about their kibble to take a chance of being attacked by the invading hordes of hungry critters. Besides, as I later learned, the varmints viewed the dog food as an open invitation to pay a visit and have a satisfying meal with their feral buddies.

The problem started late one evening when I heard my dogs making a loud commotion. I turned on the porch light and opened the front door, only to find four fat raccoons slowly sauntering away. They looked well fed and sassy, and were not frightened of me in the least. After I calmed down the dogs and the raccoons sluggishly waddled away into the darkening night, I decided to inspect the front porch. Sure enough, much of the dog food had been eaten by the overfed raccoons, but also they had spilled some onto the porch, which was soaked with raccoon saliva. I decided to scoop the remaining food up and return it to the container. Suddenly, I felt a sharp prick, and looked at my right hand and discovered a wooden splinter imbedded in the palm. Initially, I didn't think much about it, so I removed it and washed my hands off in the outside faucet. Only when I went inside my home did I realize the splinter had been lying on the porch, which was dripping in raccoon saliva, and—guess what—raccoons are carriers of rabies.

Yikes!

Immediately, I rushed to the kitchen sink and liberally scrubbed my hands with soap and water. The day was Saturday, so I planned to contact the state epidemiologist—the one who deals with this sort of problem—when his office opened on Monday, to confirm what I was already convinced of. I'd been exposed to the dreaded disease and needed to start the rabies vaccination series, the sooner the better.

Early Monday morning, after a nervous, teeth-gnashing weekend, I was up and at 'em. The minute the Oklahoma State Epidemiologist's office opened, I wanted to speak with the epidemiologist on duty.

I dialed the direct number to the office and after a few rings, a male voice answered, "Hello?"

"Hi, I'm Doctor Gary Conrad. May I talk with the State Epidemiologist?"

"Speaking. How can I help you?"

"I'm calling to see what I need to do to start the rabies immunizations."

"Tell me what happened."

"Just a few days ago, some raccoons on my front porch got into my dogs' food."

"Yes?"

"They scattered the food all over the porch, which was wet with raccoon saliva. When I picked up the food, a splinter punctured my hand."

"Were you able to get it out?"

"Yes."

"Does the site look infected?"

"No."

"Is your tetanus status up to date?"

"Yes."

"Let me be clear about this," he succinctly asked. "Were you bitten by one of the raccoons?"

"No."

"So, you believe the splinter that stuck in your hand was contaminated with raccoon saliva?

"Yes."

"Did any of the raccoons look sick?"

"No." *But how could I be certain? After all, it was nighttime.*

"Can I put you on hold for a moment? I need to check the statistics for your area."

"Good," I responded, and then I thought: *What's there to check? I was exposed to the saliva of a possibly rabid raccoon. It wouldn't be safe not to start the rabies vaccinations.*

After a few painfully long minutes, he came back on the line.

"I've checked the Logan Country area, where Guthrie is located."

"Yes?"

"And I've found there's been no rabies there for over a year. That, combined with the fact that you weren't bitten, and none of the raccoons looked sick, makes me certain you don't need the vaccine."

I felt my heart rate skyrocket. "Are you sure about this?"

"Absolutely. Goodbye."

With that I heard a click, and my savior from contracting an excruciatingly painful and probably fatal case of rabies was gone.

I felt a lump in my throat. I wondered: *Was he willing to risk my life based on statistics? What if a rabid raccoon from the next county had made a cross-country trek to pay a social visit with his friends?*

The next ten days were a living hell, and I thought about rabies nonstop. When I woke up in the morning, I thought of rabies. Throughout the day, even when I was seeing patients, rabies was on my mind. I would think as I examined a moaning patient: *You're here for a sore throat, and I'm just weeks away from an agonizing death from rabies? Give me a break.* Even when I slept, I had horrible dreams about rabies.

As might be expected, in my free time I did nonstop research and learned a tremendous amount. I discovered that the chief carriers of rabies were wild animals such as skunks, bats, foxes, coyotes and, gulp—*raccoons*!!!

My nervousness increased as I read more about the early symptoms, which were similar in many ways to influenza or other viral illnesses: fever, general weakness, aching all over and headache. Later on, as the disease progressed, other signs could appear, such as confusion, difficulty swallowing, insomnia, hallucinations, partial paralysis and hydrophobia—fear of water. Once these symptoms manifested, though, survival was rare, and death normally occurred within days. *Should I get my affairs in order?*

I knew, as did the State Epidemiologist, that rabies was easy to prevent with the vaccine. When patients show up in the emergency department with a bite from a known dog or cat, the standard of care, assuming the animal appeared to be healthy, is to quarantine the animal for ten days. If any signs of rabies develop during that period, then rabies vaccinations are started promptly.

So, since the raccoons looked healthy, I intuited that I had at least that much time before I had to start the rabies vaccinations. If the rabies virus was on that splinter, and the State Epidemiologist refused to budge, then I was destined to die a slow, miserable death, much like Old Yeller of Disney fame. As my mind wandered into fantasy land, I could picture the whole agonizing scenario:

One month from now, I'm sitting at home relaxing, having not received the rabies vaccinations. Suddenly I realize I'm feeling a little achy and having a headache. I take my temperature: 102 degrees. That night I have terrible insomnia, and the next morning I wake from my troubled sleep and realize I'm hallucinating—thinking I can see into the future. I can't believe what my visions show. *Was Donald Trump really elected to the presidency? Talk about a hellish nightmare! And surely, surely, the Cubs would never win the World Series. I must be losing my mind.*

I get out of bed, sweaty, grumpy and feeling the need to take a shower and wash off the dried sweat. I turn on the water, but as it streams out, I turn away from it, frightened, agitated, and wanting to run away—*hydrophobia!* Over the hours to come, unnatural coarse, dark brown hair begins to appear on my face and all over my body. My teeth become pointed and unnaturally stick out of my mouth like fangs, and I begin walking on all fours. I wander onto the front porch, growl at the dogs to keep them away and begin eating their food. Shortly afterward, when I return inside, I lift my right leg and pee on the couch. When my daughters try to help me, I bare my teeth and snarl at them. They call emergency medical services, and I am put in leather restraints when I try to bite one of the paramedics.

Soon, after I arrive in the emergency department, the physician realizes that I have contracted rabies. At this time, like a werewolf, I seem to have developed an unnatural, feral strength, and I break through every one of the restraints they put me in. When massive doses of Haldol and Ativan—major sedative agents—fail to control my wild, animalistic behavior, the police are summoned to the hospital to do the only humane thing they could; ending my life like our beloved Old Yeller, the police put a bullet in my head.

As I slowly die, all of my recently acquired hair slowly disappears and my teeth recede to their normal size, and, once again, like the movies, I become human again. My three daughters, all weeping and upset, fall across my now dead body and one cries out, "Why didn't they give Daddy the rabies vaccine? *Why? Why?*"

Finally, at the end of ten days of apprehension and far too many vivid imaginings, I decide it was high time to give the State Epidemiologist another try. Surely he would see the error of his ways and relent. Not that I was excited about receiving the vaccine, but it was better than dying the agonizing death I envisioned. I would finally get the vital, life-saving medicine that I needed. The cavalry—the State Epidemiologist—would arrive just in the nick of time.

I punched the numbers on the phone. Again, I heard a familiar male voice, "Hello?"

"Hi. I'm Doctor Gary Conrad. I talked to you about eight days ago. Do you remember?"

"Not exactly. Would you refresh my memory?"

"Sure. I'm the one in Guthrie who was possibly exposed to rabies after being stuck by a splinter that was contaminated with raccoon saliva."

"Oh, yes, I remember. What can I help you with today?"

"Well, today is ten days after I was exposed, and I really believe we should go ahead and start the rabies series, just to be certain."

I hear a sigh of exasperation. "Doctor, I'm 100% sure you don't need the rabies vaccinations. Just as I felt those days ago, I'm certain you will be fine."

"But . . ."

"Doctor, you won't get rabies."

"But . . ."

The line went prematurely dead, and I can't say that I blamed him.

I knew then that the time from exposure to actual, clinical rabies is usually several weeks to months, but can range from days to years. As much as I hate to confess it, I found it hard to get the concern of getting rabies out of my mind. With the tincture of time and recalling the reassuring words of the State Epidemiologist, my fears gradually diminished, and now, many years later, I am worry and rabies free.

As I look back on my own experience with nosophobia, I have a much better understanding of how people must feel who have a fear of contracting a disease. The associated emotions I felt were suffocating, constricting and panicky, with a dash of helplessness thrown into the mix. Through my own suffering, I have been able to grow and learn more not only about myself, but also about those who suffer from an irrational fear of disease, and all in all, that certainly makes worthwhile any discomfort I experienced.

Chapter 20

TIMES FOR SKEPTICISM

When I was a young pup and just starting my work in the emergency department, I tried to take what I had learned in my training and apply that wisdom to the real world of medicine. One of the most important points I had been taught by my mentors was to listen carefully to what my patients say. Most of the time, if I just pay close attention, their words will reveal what the diagnosis should be. The physical examination performed afterward is merely to confirm what I already suspected from the history.

However, there are certain instances when the health care provider has to take what the patient says with a grain of salt. In spite of my fervent desire to be as humanistic and as compassionate as possible, over the years I have adopted a set of somewhat cynical but useful rules for those occasions when my skepticism has been as high as the Goodyear blimp.

The first guideline, passed on to me by generations of knowing physicians, is the *Rule of Sixes*, which refers to alcohol consumption. Whatever quantity the patient says he drank, if the provider multiplies it by six, he'll get a closer idea of how much the patient actually had. An example of the rule is illustrated by this hypothetical, but not atypical tale. I walk into a room and discover an unshaven man lying on his stomach on the stretcher, snoring loudly and not acknowledging my entry. The entire room reeks with an odd mixture of body odor, urine and alcohol.

I say, "Sir?

Hearing no reply, I speak a lot louder, nearly yelling, "Sir?"

No response.

I decide to shake him vigorously and scream a few more times, and he finally arouses. He cracks open his bloodshot, vacant-appearing eyes, bloody saliva drooling out of the corner of his mouth.

He sputters out, "Who . . . are you?"

"I'm Doctor Gary Conrad. I'm an emergency physician at the hospital."

"How did I get to the hospital?"

"You don't remember?"

"No."

"The nurses tell me they've had difficulty keeping you awake."

"Well . . . that's because I'm tired."

"Tired?"

"Yes."

"You smell like you've been drinking. How much have you had?

He scratches his chin and mutters, "Two beers . . . or was it three?"

At this point, unbeknownst to him, he has given me valuable information. Likely, he has had twelve to eighteen beers. His alcohol level, if I choose to check it, will be sky high. The *Rule of Sixes* has rarely failed me.

Another example of when the doctor should listen with a measure of suspicion is when the patient was beaten up in a fight. Besides often being falling-down drunk, perhaps high on drugs and difficult to evaluate, for some reason the fight victims nearly always want to appear as innocent as a newborn lamb. While the physician wants to believe them, most of the time their story and what actually happened are two very different things. They just don't match. This is called the *I Was Minding My Own Business Rule*." Again, I give a fictional example.

I go into a room and ask, "Mr. Jones, what happened to you?"

The patient is sitting on the side of the bed, his face is so swollen he can barely open his eyes. The room smells like a Jack Daniel's distillery. With an edge to his voice, he says, "I was beaten up . . . can't you tell?"

"Oh, I can tell. How did it happen?"

"You won't believe it. I was sitting in a lawn chair on the front porch of my home, minding my own business and reading the Bible, when a car drove up in front of my home—"

I shake my head in disbelief and force myself to say, "Really?"

"Oh yes. I had just finished reading the line from Psalms, 'The Lord is my Shepherd; I shall not want,' when four men popped out of a car with tire tools. And this," he said pointing to his face, "is what they did to me."

"How much did you have to drink?"

"Drink? Me?"

"Yes, you."

"Oh, I never drink much when I read the Bible. Maybe three or four beers?"

In this situation, it's a good idea to combine the *Rule of Sixes* with the *I Was Minding My Own Business Rule*. Whatever the truth might be, he will be treated the same whether he is the perpetrator or not. But, is it any wonder that, after hearing this same sort of yarn too many times to count over the years that many emergency physicians and nurses become jaded? How could they not?

Another axiom about doubtful listening, which most emergency physicians know quite well, is *The More They Complain, the*

Less Likely Anything Is Wrong Rule. These are the most frustrating patients of all, ones who say yes to whatever I ask. When I pick up the chart, I know I'm in trouble when I read the nursing notes and the information says, "Patient complains of chest pain, positive review of systems." In other words, the nurse is warning me to get ready for more complaints than I could ever imagine. The interview might go something like this:

"Mrs. McGillicutty, you're having chest pain?"

"Yes."

"How long had it been going on?"

"Ten years."

At this stage, one wonders: *Why is someone coming to the emergency department for a complaint that has been going on this long?* Unfortunately, it happens all the time, and hearing multiple long-standing complaints is not uncommon.

"Why did you come in today?"

"It got worse."

"What's it like?"

"It's a tight, squeezing pain. I feel like I can't breathe."

"What does your doctor think about this?"

"I don't have a doctor."

This answer holds no surprise. Access to a primary care provider is a continued, longstanding problem. "Have you seen anyone about this?"

"I've been to seven different ERs. No one can find out what's going on."

"Anything else?"

"Yes, I have a headache."

"How long have you been having this headache?"

"Five years."

"Does your stomach hurt?"

"Oh yes. From top to bottom."

"When did this start?"

"When I was five years old."

I do all I can to keep a straight face. "I see you've got a lot going on. Let's run some tests—"

"But Doctor, I'm not done. My legs hurt all the time and I can barely walk. Both of my arms tingle, and my neck and back are killing me. I've got a sore on my right foot that won't go away, and I'm nervous and depressed—all at the same time. Oh, and yes, I need some pain medicine now!"

Obviously, this interview is going nowhere. After examining the patient and not-so-gracefully exiting the room, I order a battery of tests to make sure that nothing too serious is actually going on. Most of the time, though, these workups are stone-cold normal, simply because the most likely cause of odd, multisystem, unrelated complaints is psychiatric in origin.

In my younger and more flippant days, when this sort of interview took place, I would often ask the probing question, "Do your stools glow in the dark?" knowing that a positive answer nearly always guaranteed the patient was completely obsessed with health issues.

When I asked this, sometimes the patient would look at me like I was crazy—a good sign—and at other times their faces would light up, and they would give me an enthusiastic "Yes!" as if they were thinking: *Why has no one ever asked me that before?* In retrospect, as ridiculous as the question was, the answer and the way the patient gave it rendered valuable information.

A final truism is the *Rule of the Vague Complaint.* When I see a complaint on the chart that looks to be dull or unimaginative, I wonder whether or not that is the real reason the patient has come to see me. This occurs because the real problem, at least in the patient's own mind, is too embarrassing to tell the triage nurse, and he will give a false, everyday complaint just to get through the door. Years ago, this case really happened.

I entered the room and saw an eighteen-year-old man sitting

across from me on the table. I sat down and said, "Hi, I'm Doctor Gary Conrad. I see on the chart you're having pain in your right arm?"

"Yes, it's been bothering me for some time."

"Okay."

At this point he motioned me to move close to the table. I stood up and walked up to him. He whispered, "I've actually got a discharge."

"From your penis?"

"Yes, it's been going on for two weeks. It's yellow and green, and it hurts to pee."

"Unprotected intercourse?"

"Yes."

After I left the room, I ordered a culture and a gram stain, and quickly indentified the problem: gonorrhea. Of course, I treated him also for Chlamydia, just in case he happened to have a concurrent infection. He was given a shot of Rocephin and a prescription for an oral antibiotic with instructions to follow up at the State Health Department for HIV testing. He was to abstain from intercourse until he was determined to be clear of the disease, and he should use condoms to prevent re-infection.

Four months later I was working in the emergency department when I picked up a chart that said, "Right arm pain." I walked into the room and found the same young man sitting in a chair.

I knowingly asked, "Discharge come back?"

He grinned at my understanding and answered, "Yes."

I returned his smile and found myself more-than-a-little amazed at the synchronicity of it all; how I happened to be the emergency physician that treated him beforehand. As might be guessed, the patient's evaluation once again confirmed the diagnosis of gonorrhea, and he was prescribed medications as before.

At discharge—pun intended—I admonished him anew to use condoms to protect himself, but I had the distinct feeling that my recommendation fell on deaf ears.

One of the greatest challenges for us, as emergency physicians, is to keep an unbiased, caring approach as we go from patient
to patient. The difficulty occurs when we are faced over and over
with misleading or intentionally deceptive patients, ones that can
color our perspective and make us cynical if we're not careful.

For me, I strive to take a fresh outlook into the room every
time I see a new patient, and try to give that person the benefit of
the doubt, no matter how odd or bewildering the patients were that
preceded him or her. While certainly all of us—whether emergency
physicians or not—experience times for legitimate skepticism, perhaps as individuals we can weave love, kindness and understanding
into these situations and maybe, just maybe, change them in some
small way for the better.

Chapter 21

VERMIN

D octors and nursing personnel are more-than-occasionally exposed to different kinds of vermin, ones that would make the average person either want to run away screaming or perch on the nearest chair. The responsibility to deal with pests of all kinds comes with the job, though, and without question these foul creatures make working in an emergency department more interesting. Sadly enough, if a patient's home is teeming with noxious critters, it's guaranteed that they'll bring a representative sample with them to the hospital. The prototypical example of this phenomenon is the eighty-plus year old person, usually a woman—because women live longer than men—who lives with more cats than Snow White has dwarves.

EMS (Emergency Medical Services) despises calls to these homes more than any other. Such residences, without fail, reek with the odor of old urine mixed with cigarette smoke, and invariably the kitchen is piled full of dirty dishes, many with decaying mounds of food on them. The buzzing of swarms of flies comes close to drowning out the volume of the TV, which is turned up high and is frequently tuned to a soap opera rerun.

The moment EMS personnel arrive at such scenes, besides the numerous pesky flies, they discover more roaches skittering about than there are Packer fans in Green Bay. Multiple torn-open bags of kitty litter and cat food are often stacked along the hallways, contents spilling on the urine-soaked carpet, barely giving EMS enough room to enter with their stretcher. To top it all off, the thermostat in these wretched dens is usually set to at least eighty degrees, no matter the temperature outside, making all who enter miserably uncomfortable—like they've entered the sauna from Hell.

When a patient from such a dwelling comes to see us, one of the unwelcome guests can be maggots. As many times as I've encountered them over the years, one would have supposed that I would be used to them, but no one could ever get accustomed to these disgusting, worm-like creatures that thrive on rotten flesh. Even seasoned nurses, male and female alike, scream with disgust as they pull the socks off a patient's feet, and the maggots come flying out like they were shot from Roman candles.

Not that maggots are necessarily a bad thing—they aren't. I fondly recall when I was a medical student and read the book by William A. Nolen, M.D, titled *The Making of a Surgeon*, which was originally published in 1968. In the book, during Nolen's surgical residency, he discovered that when homeless people arrived at the hospital harboring maggots, invariably their wounds were as clean as a countertop in Howard Hughes' kitchen. This observation led Nolen to further investigate the possible use of maggots as a tool in wound care. He decided to keep a stock of maggots in his locker to apply to patients' wounds that appeared necrotic or infected. The study was going swimmingly until his stored maggots metamorphosed from larvae into flies, and they buzzed out of his locker and invaded the hospital, terrorizing patients and health care providers alike. As I recall, an exterminator was called in to clean up the aftermath, and, after Nolen was reprimanded, his monumental scientific experiment was put on ice, never to grace the halls of his institution again. In more recent years, though, maggot therapy has become an accepted treatment option for cleaning wounds of dead tissue in certain situations.

Another common unwanted invader is head or body lice. Except for maggots, no vermin causes more disgust among nursing personnel. As is well known, lice are parasitic insects that reside on the clothes or bedding of infected persons, and they migrate to the skin to feed on their host's blood when it's chowtime. Usually, lice are only seen in homeless patients or those who are unable, for whatever reason, to bathe, wear clean clothes, and sleep in laundered bedding. Lice are spread by direct contact with an infected person or their bedclothes, so the nurses' anxiety about caring for such patients becomes understandable. No one wants to carry lice home to paracitize family members. In the emergency department, lice are much more common than maggots, and they are often discovered by finding nits on the hair of the patients, or, heaven forbid, seeing bugs crawling around once their clothes are removed. Once lice are recognized, the patient is treated with a good scrubbing and a pediculicide, a chemical agent that kills lice. No one wants to perform this less-than-appealing task, but the nursing staff grit their teeth and do what's necessary.

In keeping with the theme of this somewhat revolting chapter, on one occasion an older woman in her 80s presented to the emergency department with what we affectionately call a "suitcase sign." In other words, she had already made the decision that she will be staying in the hospital, come Hell or high water, and no one, whether doctor, nurse, case manager, or administrator, was going to convince her otherwise.

This particular patient was medically complex, and one of her suitcases was devoted to carrying an enormous number of pill bottles. When the nurse opened the suitcase to make a list of her prescriptions, a swarm of hungry black cockroaches exploded from the bag, seeking their next meal, or perhaps just pleased to be given a chance at freedom. As the insects crawled everywhere, the patient exclaimed, "You can't get rid of those things, so you might as well feed them." Apparently she had been doing just that. The next thirty minutes were spent finding and eliminating the nasty bugs.

Another time, on a frigid, snowy evening, an obese, elderly woman arrived with a complaint of chest pain. She was wrapped in multiple layers of clothing, and she wore a long, thick, black coat, one that was covered with—you guessed it—cat hair. In keeping with the ancient medical axiom, "If you can't see it, you can't diagnose it," the nurses began to peel off her clothes. Three layers down, a small bloody, furry object burst forth, falling right at the feet of one of the nurses, who screamed and leaped back.

When the nurses screwed up their courage to take a closer look, they discovered a squished mouse, freshly killed, guts hanging out of its mouth. Apparently the mouse was in the patient's clothing when the patient unexpectedly rolled over on top of it.

In all of the cases listed above, a call to APS (Adult Protective Services) was generated in order to perform a home evaluation, and I suppose that many of those patients were eventually placed in long term care. Most that live in such deplorable, unsanitary conditions likely have either dementia or psychiatric problems and urgently need medical and social assistance.

In dealing with these tough-to-treat patients, I continue to be amazed at the commitment of the nurses that work day-to-day with them. As a physician, while I am involved with a number of challenging problems, my primary duties are making diagnoses and prescribing medications. The nurses, to their credit, perform the nitty-gritty, steamy, sticky, in-your-face labor. Anyone who might doubt that nurses are indeed dedicated angels of mercy need look no further than those who treat patients afflicted by vermin.

In assessing my career as an emergency physician, if I am considered to be successful, much of the credit belongs to the nurses, paramedics, EMTs, and other health care providers with whom I work. Certainly, providing quality medical care is a team effort, and no health care practitioners in emergency medicine achieve success as solo actors—no one.

Especially when vermin are involved.

Chapter 22

DOCTOR STEREOTYPES

Most medical doctors fit into a particular mold, depending upon their specialty, and often they can be identified by certain, distinguishing characteristics. Take for example, the general surgeon, who is expected to have the skills and knowledge to perform a wide range of procedures, from breast surgery to removing cancer from the colon. The average general surgeon is aggressive, a quick decision maker, clean cut—usually—and often a man. He wears surgical scrubs everywhere, as if to say—*Look at me! I'm a doctor!*—and could never be accused of radiating peace and tranquility. One will never find a surgeon meditating in the doctor's lounge between cases, and under no circumstance will this dynamo be involved in a lengthy, tearful, touchy-feely conversation. Rather, he has a tendency to be hyperactive, high-strung, and continually on the prowl to do something to show off his superiority and machismo. After all, he's a doer, and action is his stock-in-trade. If a doctor betrays an involuntary nervous twitch, certainly a manifestation of his near-manic, bottled-up energy, he's bound to be a surgeon. For the prototypical surgeon, making a deep incision is the answer to almost any problem that faces the world.

Internal medicine physicians present themselves in a manner easy to recognize. The most cerebral of all the specialists, they are the doctors who are called upon to solve the puzzling diagnostic problems that are beyond the comprehension of mere mortal physicians. Never ask an internist to make a quick decision, because this doctor needs plenty of unfettered time to consider *ad nauseum* every angle of the problem. If the internist is a man, even the selection of underwear in the morning poses a major undertaking. As he stares at his dresser drawers, he asks himself: *Should I wear my plaid boxers or my white briefs?* Or, if a woman, picking out her clothes can present a similar conundrum: *What outfit would look best on me, the black suit or the white blouse with grey slacks?* Typically, internists, whether male or female, dress stylishly and conservatively, oftentimes wearing a starched, medium-length white coat to demonstrate how professional they are. Probably the best image that describes an internist is the statue, "The Thinker," by Auguste Rodin. No one in the world is smarter than an internist, and they know it—though perhaps Einstein and da Vinci came close. Physicians in this specialty are the ones most likely to work crossword puzzles with an ink pen and be members of the local Mensa society. Internists don't smoke because they know a dozen fatal maladies caused by smoking, but if they did, they would hang a carved mahogany pipe from the corners of their mouths, puffing away and contemplating the complex and mind-boggling problems that they must solve to treat their patients.

A physician wearing a bow tie or a T-shirt, has a ninety-nine percent chance of being a pediatrician. If the same doctor is hard of hearing or wearing a hearing aid, again, that confirms he takes care of little ones. Years of treating irritable, snotty-nosed children screaming at the top of their lungs have finally taken their toll on his now stiffened and sclerotic eardrums. Pediatricians are also likely to have abnormally large arm muscles in proportion to the rest of their body, Popeye-like, simply because, on an ongoing basis, they have to keep thrashing, wild-eyed children from flopping off the examination table onto the floor while their mothers are distracted by their other shrieking munchkins.

If the doctor is female, always wears scrubs and squints a lot in the light of day, then she has to be an OB/GYN physician. She is accustomed to performing her duties in the after-midnight hours, because that seems to be the period of time when most women deliver. If she's not squinting and seems rested, obviously she has learned from all her years of nighttime deliveries, and now she induces her patients early in the morning so they will likely give birth during the day. If the doctor is popping antacids nonstop, this is another give-away that she is an OB/GYN physician. The day-to-day pressure of delivering babies, where hair-raising crises occur on a more-than-occasional basis, makes indigestion and even ulcer disease a likely occupational hazard.

A physician who has the physical characteristics of a mole or gopher, with a long, pointed nose and grown-out fingernails, and avoids going outside unless it's a cloudy, dark day, rest assured he is a radiologist. He spends his entire existence sitting in a darkened room looking at x-rays on a monitor, and while on occasion he will actually speak to a patient, most of the time he stays in his office staring at images as they cross before his emotionless, pale face. If one is uncertain whether the doctor is an OB/GYN or a radiologist, the best indicator is conversational skills. The OB/GYN is adept at chatting with patients—it's her job—while the radiologist barely musters the will to mutter out a word or two. He went into radiology for a reason; he doesn't like to interact with people and prefers to be by himself, sequestered away in a dark, secluded corner of the hospital.

Other informative tidbits: when the doctor is tall, muscular, and wears tight clothes to show off his amazing body, he surely is an orthopedist. If he pops his knuckles a lot, this is another sign, as he loves any noise that sounds like bones crunching. If a physician looks at someone with a prolonged, piercing gaze and asks about his or her mother, certainly she is a psychiatrist. The physician who smiles all the time has to be the family practitioner, whose motto is "What—Me Worry?" like *Mad Magazine's* Alfred E. Neuman. He doesn't have a care in the world, as he knows that the moment his patients become critically ill, he can turn them over to a brilliant internal medicine doctor who will deal with their nitty-gritty, life-threatening issues. If the doctor standing in line in the grocery store has the faint odor of formaldehyde emanating from her, drowning out any hint of perfume, no question she is a pathologist, who, like the radiologist, has a disdain for being around anyone who lives and breathes. After all, it suits the pathologist just fine that a corpse cannot talk, much less complain. The dead bodies she dissects don't whine about the side effects of their medications, how their families don't appreciate them, how they can't pay their medical bills or how they were mistreated as children.

Emergency physicians, the group I know and understand the best, tend to be a unique lot, and are best described as a Heinz 57 mixture of the specialists mentioned above. As opposed to surgeons and internists, no specific appearances define them. One can be very GQ and polished in his look, while another might have long hair and a disarrayed beard and moustache, wearing casual clothes to the hospital before changing into scrubs. A number of emergency physicians, like the surgeons, have a short-fused, aggressive edge about them, while others have an aura like that of Tiny Tim, emanating the feeling that they could easily pick up a ukulele and comfortably sing "Tiptoe Through the Tulips" in a lilting, high-pitched vibrato.

While the variety that is found among emergency doctors has a far greater range than any other specialty, they can still be identified by several defining attributes. First, they have a tendency to be constantly nervous, simply because of the unpredictable nature of their practice. The emergency department is a random place, prone to chaos, and one moment a physician can be sitting and relaxing, sharing jokes with the nursing staff, and in the next instant, someone teetering on the brink of death is rushed through the front door, requiring immediate intervention.

Adding to the pressure, the emergency physician is expected to have some modicum of skill in all the different specialty areas—no exceptions. The internist has no concern about dealing with a sick child, because she's not expected to know anything about pediatric illnesses. The OB/GYN is not required to be familiar with anything about heart attacks; it's outside of her area of expertise. The radiologist is not expected to diagnose skin cancer—that's what dermatologists do.

But the emergency physician has no excuse. He might not have the specific proficiency of a specialist, but he must have savvy and be exceptionally good at dealing with whatever problem he may be faced with at any given moment. Indeed, an emergency physician has to know something about everything, because in any given shift, he may have to treat a woman who's delivering a baby, a man with a gunshot wound, a teenager who crashed his motorcycle and has multiple broken bones and internal injuries, a woman suffering from a debilitating case of vertigo, and even a senior citizen who fell and might have a brain hemorrhage.

So, the next time doctors are introduced—assuming they are not a PhD, a chiropractor or a veterinarian—take a stab at trying to figure out the specialty of each. While exceptions exist to every stereotypical rule, with the guidelines listed above, I believe most can figure out the specialty of the physician who is standing in front of them, unless, of course, he or she is an emergency physician.

Then, all bets are off.

Chapter 23

A CASE OF GRAVITY

Taking care of the elderly who have fallen is a constant challenge in the practice of emergency medicine. In contrast, when younger patients stumble and hurt themselves, the cause is generally straightforward and the injuries are usually minor. After performing a history and physical examination, x-rays are typically ordered and assessed, and the patient can often be sent on his or her way with instructions for appropriate follow up care.

When senior citizens collapse, the first question to be asked is, "Why did you fall?" If they simply tripped, often on an area rug or a rambunctious family pet, their assessment is not such a conundrum. The problem arises when older patients say they passed out, their balance hasn't been good lately, or they fell because of severe dizziness. The cause of such episodes can vary greatly. Could it be a heart attack? A stroke? An electrolyte abnormality? A blockage in their carotid arteries? Bleeding from somewhere in their gastrointestinal tract? A medication reaction? A cardiac arrhythmia? A urinary tract infection? The list goes on, and can range anywhere from something minor to the deadly serious.

Adding to the complexity, many members of the older population have dementia, and, depending upon the severity of their com-
promised mental acuity, the histories that older persons give cannot
be totally trusted. They may say they don't hurt anywhere, but often
the physician cannot be certain about injuries from a fall without a
thorough laboratory and x-ray evaluation. For example, if someone
with severe dementia is discovered on the nursing home floor after a
fall, and the patient arrives in the emergency department moaning in
pain, injuries are impossible to sort out by history and physical exam
alone. Often a pan scan, also known as a whole-body CAT scan, is required to rule out life-threatening injuries. Complexity is the name
of the game in caring for folks in their golden years, at least part of
the reason a high percentage of patients' health care costs occur in the
last months of their lives.

An aged patient who has suffered a fall has never been my
favorite type of case to assess. The elderly nearly always require
time-consuming workups that take hours to complete, and, even
after applying the latest up-to-date technological tools, frequently I
still don't have a definitive explanation for the cause. When I talk
with concerned family members, the conversation commonly goes
something like this:

"Hi, I'm Doctor Gary Conrad. I met you earlier when your
father was brought in. You're his daughter?"

"I am," said a concerned, gray-haired woman, who appears to
be in her sixties. "What did you find out?"

"Well, as you know, I ordered an extensive evaluation: an
EKG, chest x-ray, blood work, urinalysis, as well at CAT scans of his
head, neck, chest and abdomen and pelvis."

"And?" she asks, her eyebrows rising ever so slightly.

"They were all normal," I reply.

"Then what caused my father to pass out?"

"I don't know, but I'd like to contact his internist and keep your father in the hospital for further evaluation."

I see a look of frustration cross her face. "That's fine. But after all you've done, do you believe while he is in the hospital, we'll eventually discover why he fainted and fell?"

"It's hard to say. The cause of syncope can often be elusive, but I'm certain your doctor will do the best that she can."

"Oh, I'm sure of that," she responds, a look of dissatisfaction in her eyes.

Over the years, I have had a tendency to sigh in annoyance as ambulance after ambulance has brought in confused, elderly patients who have fallen, many with blood-saturated dressings covering scalp or facial lacerations. One day, though, after a personal, first-hand experience with going to the ground, my attitude about taking care of such patients took an abrupt about-face.

I love visiting New York City, and every so often my wife, Sheridan, and I travel to the Big Apple so I can attend a medical conference and keep up to date on all the latest happenings in emergency medicine.

What's not to love about Manhattan? The art museums are among the best in the world, the Metropolitan Museum of Art, the Museum of Modern Art, the Guggenheim Museum—designed by Frank Lloyd Wright—and my personal favorite, the Neue Museum, which houses a breathtaking painting by Gustav Klimt, titled, *Portrait of Adele Bloch-Bauer I.*

Besides the art museums, the gustatory scene is at least as wonderful, and while vegetarian restaurants in Oklahoma are as rare as penguins living in the Sahara, they are plentiful in New York City, allowing delectable dining experiences for those who prefer a plant-based diet.

In addition, the entertainment is second to none. After spending a good part of the day listening to lectures on varied topics in emergency medicine, a refreshing break comes with taking in a

Broadway or off-Broadway play later that night. Also, as one walks the bustling, crowded streets, the opportunity arises to appreciate the drumbeat of a vibrant, active city. While I prefer not to have a steady diet of such a *milieu*, in small doses, the atmosphere is stimulating and captivating.

With this in mind, during the middle of one of our adventures to New York City, Sheridan planned to travel by rail and visit a close friend who lived in New Hampshire, leaving me for a day to enjoy the city by myself. After the conference finished that sunny afternoon, I saw her onto a train that left from Pennsylvania Station, which lies underneath Madison Square Garden.

Later, as I was happily strolling along in the Times Square area, not far from my hotel, I found myself distracted by many different sights: people dressed like the Statue of Liberty, Batman, Superman and Spiderman, Tibetan monks asking for donations, vendors of all sorts peddling their wares, street dancers gyrating to rap music, landscape artists creating vibrant scenes using spray paint, huge flashing neon billboards that nearly blot out the sky, people from many different countries gawking in awe—just like I was—at the undulating scene before them. For an Okie who is not used to this sort of environment, the sights created complete sensory overload.

As I turned my head back and forth, taking in the staggering spectacle, I must've looked like one of those bobble-head dogs people put on top of their car dashboard. Unfortunately, I wasn't paying close-enough attention to where I was walking. Just ahead of me, a street light turned green, and I hustled to the curb that I might catch the light and join the stream of crossing pedestrians. I hadn't planned on the unexpectedly deep drop-off onto the street from the sidewalk, and to my dismay, I lost my balance and tripped, flying head-over-heels, my head striking the pavement with a crunch that sounded like a dropped watermelon. The sacks I was carrying launched from my arms like errant rockets into the crowd.

I heard several bystanders yell out, "Are you okay?" as I

momentarily lay on the asphalt.

Embarrassed, I quickly popped up and said, "I'm fine."

At that moment, I felt warm, sticky blood streaming onto my face from a wound on my left forehead, and I wiped it from my eyes, still a bit stunned and feeling rather silly. Since I was unable to look directly at the injury, I wondered whether or not I needed stitches.

Witnesses to the fall kindly gathered up my belongings, and one of them, a young Asian woman said, "We live here, and nearby, just down the street, is a police station. Shall we walk you over there?"

With my nod, they led me along. As I unsteadily stumbled through the front door of the station, a policeman greeted me and asked, "What happened?"

I sheepishly answered, "I fell off a curb."

"Would you like me to call an ambulance?"

"I'm not sure. Does it look like my head needs to be sutured?"

He peered closely at my oozing forehead. "No, I don't think so. It just looks like a deep scrape, but I'd be happy to call an ambulance so the paramedics can check you."

I still had my wits about me, so I quickly assessed my condition. I wasn't knocked unconscious. I had only a slight headache. My neck didn't hurt. I had no nausea or vomiting, and I didn't take any anticoagulants, making the risk of a brain bleed less likely. I thought I would be fine.

"No, sir," I said. "My hotel is nearby. I believe I can walk there by myself."

"Are you sure about that?"

"Yes, I'm a physician," I calmly replied, "and I know the danger signs to watch for. I believe I'll be okay."

"Whatever you like," he responded, with a look of doubt on his face.

And with that bit of bravado, I turned to the small group that had assisted me. I took my carefully gathered-up bags from them and sincerely said, "Thank you—thank you ever so much."

"You're welcome," they answered, just before they smiled and turned away.

After I left the station, I walked the three or four blocks back to my hotel, and, judging from the horrified stares of other pedestrians I passed, I must have looked like a cast member of a chainsaw massacre movie. In fact, when I got on the elevator to my floor, one woman asked, "Are you in makeup?"

I grinned and said, "I wish I was. No, it's the real thing. I took a fall just a bit ago."

Other passengers in the elevator murmured sympathetically.

After getting off on my floor, I stumbled toward my room and was greeted by a hotel security guard who happened to be walking the halls.

"What happened?" he asked.

"Just a little tumble."

"Looks like more than a little one," he said as he shook his head.

Now in front of my room, he opened the door with his keys and led me inside. He said, "I'll be back in a minute."

I immediately went to the mirror in the bathroom and inspected the injury. While the wound would not require sutures, it was deep and still bleeding. I could see the bloody impressions where the rough pavement had dug into my forehead.

I heard a knock at the door, and after opening it, I saw the guard, his hands full of bandaging material.

"I thought you might need this," he said as he sidled past me and placed them on my bathroom counter.

I reached for my wallet. "How much do I owe you?"

"Nothing," he replied.

Tears came into my eyes as I once again found myself saying, "Thank you."

"I'm glad to help."

When he closed the door as he left, I went about the business of stripping off my blood-stained clothes and hopping into the shower to wash off the dried blood and cleanse the areas that were still bleeding. I was looking forward to leaving behind my current image of a Halloween ghoul.

The next afternoon Sheridan returned from New Hampshire, and she was appalled at how nasty the wound looked on my forehead. She immediately walked to a nearby drug store and purchased bandages to replenish the ones the security guard had given me. I suspected the pockmarked wound would take a long time to heal, but with her help and care, I was certainly on my way to recovery.

The following day we happened to see the security guard who had assisted me. After I pointed him out to her, she walked up to him and said, "Thank you for taking care of my husband."

"I was happy to do it," he answered with a smile.

As we waved goodbye, I knew I would always be grateful to him and the pedestrians who assisted me at my time of great need. I then realized that the commonly-held myth of New Yorkers being rude and aloof is simply not true. No matter how crusty they seem on the outside, on the inside, as Neil Young once sang, beat hearts of gold.

In the months that followed my fall in New York City, I never developed any complications. No headaches, blood clots, dizziness—no problems whatsoever. The scar took a number of months to resolve, and now it's barely visible. I feel most blessed; the end result could have been so much worse.

One inspiration I received from my stumbling episode in New York City was a renewed sense of the humanity we share with each other. Most in our society willingly help others, and nowhere was that better demonstrated than in the aftermath of my curbside swan dive. I find myself grateful to be alive and wanting to be of service, not just in the practice of emergency medicine, but also by extending a helping hand to others in times of need.

Another outcome of my fall has been a newfound respect for the plight of seniors who've taken a tumble, and no longer do I sigh in resignation when they come rolling in on a stretcher through the doors of the emergency department. Granted, as far as my fall was concerned, I was not a confused, elderly person with complicated and tough-to-disentangle problems. As all emergency physicians know, the risk of falling and hurting ourselves increases dramatically with aging, especially as our balance becomes more precarious. While that's a sobering thought, I am certain there will always be health care providers who will offer compassionate treatment to us, no matter the circumstances. None of us have reason to fear.

We're all in this together.

Chapter 24

THE SCAPEGOAT

The practice of medicine can be called the journey of the unexpected. Every successful case has to be taken with a grain of salt, simply because no matter how heroic or admirable a physician's achievements have been in the past, lying in wait are patients who will not do well, ones who will die or become disabled in spite of the doctor's best efforts. The greatest triumph is often followed by the greatest failure, and vice versa.

In light of this, to maintain one's sanity, the physician should follow one of the precepts from Buddhism's Middle Way, the rejection of extremes, and remain emotionally dispassionate, resolute and calm. Don't get too thrilled by successes or too depressed about failures. In medicine, as in life, both are bound to happen.

In the residency years, to minimize the failures, the microscope on patient care is turned up to an extremely high level, and every move made by the fledgling doctor is monitored and scrutinized by the attending physicians and the senior residents. This happens for the greater good, as any slip-ups by younger physicians are nearly always caught by those who supervise them. The beneficiary is the patient, who is given the benefit of many minds and perspectives in the process of the individual's care.

Because of this meticulous oversight, the expectation for flawless excellence is high in the training settings. Nothing less than perfection is acceptable—no matter how unattainable this lofty standard is. Unfortunately, when the physician falls short of this ideal, it can lead to an attempt to divert blame to a colleague.

Once, I was the target of such an event, and while I felt viscerally wounded at the time, the pain has now faded into a distant, yet still tangible, memory.

My first year of residency in family practice moved inexorably along. I never had the feeling of how fast time was flying, rather, each day seemed to last an eternity, and I felt like a worm trying to complete a marathon. As I slowly inched my way through the days, I knew the end would eventually come to this intense segment of my life, yet, somehow it seemed it never would.

The OB/GYN rotation, though, in spite of the long hours and a number of gut-wrenching experiences, was going better than most. I had performed well during my brief tenure in labor and delivery, and one day, when I was making rounds with my fellow residents, the OB/GYN chief resident, Doctor Abraham Jennings, pulled me to the side.

"Gary," he said. "You're approaching the end of this rotation. Have you enjoyed it?"

"Yes, very much."

"I've talked with the attending, and because you have carried out your duties so admirably, we'd like to reward you tomorrow by letting you perform a cesarean section."

I was shocked, yet I blurted out, "That sounds great!" In training programs, one never turns down the opportunity to perform a procedure.

Seeing the look of concern on my face, he said, "I know you've never done one before, but don't worry. I will be at your side and will walk you through it. Nothing will go wrong, I promise you."

I gulped and said, "Thanks, Abe."

"You'll do great," he reassured me. "Of that I'm certain."

As I drove to my apartment that evening, I felt thrilled to have this chance, but later I became more than a little anxious. Seeing cesarean sections performed was one thing, but actually doing one? I felt a sudden tug in my gut.

The next morning, I stood in the operating room facing my senior resident. Lying between us on the operating room table was the prepped and draped abdomen of a full-term pregnant patient. We were gloved and cloaked in sterile gowns, while the anesthesiologist, who had earlier administered epidural anesthesia, sat on a stool at the head of the bed, carefully watching the patient's airway and vital signs. A pediatrics resident hovered behind us, standing next to an infant warmer, waiting to receive the newborn baby.

Abe asked the anesthesiologist, "Are we ready to start?"

With his nod, Abe said to me, "Okay, before we begin, tell me why we are performing a cesarean section on this patient."

I responded, "She has had two previous pregnancies, and both required cesarean sections. We are performing this one to prevent the possibility of uterine rupture, which could occur if we allowed her to deliver vaginally."

"What is the risk of that happening?"

"Less than one percent, but with the associated chance of maternal and fetal death, it's not worth the risk to deliver her vaginally."

"Correct. Now, go ahead and make your incision across the lower abdomen. What is that called?"

"A Pfannenstiel incision."

"Precisely."

At that point, under Abe's watchful eyes, I made the incision

through the skin of the lower abdomen and followed his further instructions meticulously, being careful not to puncture the bladder,
dissecting through the tissue layers until the uterus was revealed.

"Now," he said, "the uterus is very thin at this stage of pregnancy. Make a superficial horizontal incision in the inferior aspect
of the uterus with your scalpel, and I will bluntly dissect it with my
hands to enlarge the opening."

Following his instructions, I made a little cut in the lower
part of the uterus, with a resultant gush of yellow-colored amniotic
fluid. Abe then placed his hands in the small, incised hole and carefully teased it open until it was large enough for delivery.

"Done," he said. "Now let's have a baby."

With his words, I carefully placed my hands inside the uterus
and secured the baby's head. With gentle traction, I delivered first
the head, then the shoulders, followed by the rest of the baby. I suctioned the secretions from the baby's mouth and nose, and with that
he began to robustly cry. While no one could see my face through
the mask, I broke into a smile.

"Clamp the cord," Abe instructed, "and hand the baby over
to the pediatrician. She'll take it from there."

I gave the bellowing newborn to her, and she quickly placed
it under an infant warmer. There she dried the screaming bundle of
joy with a small, green blanket. She pulled a stethoscope from her
neck and listened to the heart and lungs. "Everything looks good,"
she said.

"Great," Abe said. "Now, Doctor Conrad, deliver the placenta from the uterus and inspect it carefully for any defects. We can't
leave any part of it behind in the uterus."

Using cautious traction, I tugged on the umbilical cord, and
when the placenta separated from the uterus, I removed it and examined it carefully. The placenta was intact. I said, "It seems fine."

"Good," Abe said. "Now, pull the uterus out of her abdominal cavity and repair the uterine incision that you made. Once you've

done that, I want you to suture up the abdominal incision."

"Yes, sir," I said.

He added, "We've still got a lot to do here before we can call it a day, but so far, so good. By the way, great job, Doctor."

"Thank you, Doctor Jennings," I said, appreciatively. It was one of the happiest, most satisfying moments of my life.

A week later, one of my fellow residents, Ron, approached me from behind and tapped me on the back of my shoulder. I turned to face him, and from the odd look in his eyes, I could tell that something wasn't quite right.

"Gary," he questioned, "do you remember the patient . . . the baby you delivered by cesarean section?"

"Yes," I said, concerned, knowing that when someone starts with the words, 'Do you remember the patient . . .,' rarely was it good news.

"Were you aware that the baby became ill two days after delivery?"

"Well, yes, I heard he developed a fever and required IV antibiotics."

Ron paused for a moment and said, "I wish I didn't have to tell you this, but you need to know the baby died late last night."

"Oh, no!" I exclaimed, inhaling deeply. "What happened?"

"The autopsy results are still pending, but the cultures indicated that the baby died from group B strep sepsis."

"Dammit!" I blurted out.

He added, "Next week, they are going to hold an M & M—morbidity and mortality—conference on the case, just in case you want to attend."

I replied, "I'll definitely be there."

Five days later, a cluster of thirty or so physicians wearing white and blue lab coats sat restlessly in the hospital conference room, sipping coffee and waiting for the meeting to begin. M & M conferences were not happy occasions, as they were never called to pat someone on the back for making an amazing diagnosis. Rather, a doctor had likely made a medical error, which led to a bad outcome, and incumbent on the medical staff was the responsibility to further investigate the details. I selected a place toward the back of the room, and Abe joined me in the seat to my left.

The dull murmur of idle chatter paused to dead silence as the pediatric attending, Doctor Garrison, gingerly wobbled into the room, supported by a black, wooden cane. He was slender, in his 70s, and had short white hair and a moustache, with black-framed glasses. Wearing a medium-length, light-blue lab coat, he grimly stood at a lectern before the attendees. The pediatricians at the hospital always wore blue, I supposed, in hope that children would not be as frightened as they might be when confronted with a sterile white one.

Doctor Garrison spoke to one of the residents sitting near the entrance to the room. "Please close the door, and make certain it stays that way."

That accomplished, Doctor Garrison cleared his throat and addressed the audience. "Welcome to the M & M conference. As most of you know, the purpose of this gathering is to perform a peer review of possible mistakes made in patient care. If we can learn from supposed missteps made by our colleagues, repeating this same error would be less likely in the future. Let me remind you that the proceedings of this meeting are confidential, and the purpose is improved patient care, not to punish a colleague in any way. Any questions before we proceed?"

Hearing no response, he looked into the front row and said, "Doctor Phillips, as our chief resident in pediatrics, would you please present the case?"

"I'd be glad to," said a corpulent, blue-coated young woman with short black hair. She rose and replaced Doctor Garrison behind the lectern, while Doctor Garrison took her seat on the first row.

She pulled a folder from her right hand and opened it on the slanted top of the wooden lectern. She said, "Justin Edwards was born by cesarean section at our hospital twelve days ago. The procedure was uncomplicated and the mother had no temperature beforehand. The infant was bottle-fed in the nursery and was on Similac formula. On the second day after delivery, at 23:10 the nurse noticed the baby was somewhat irritable. The child had no vomiting, diarrhea, cough or fever, but the nurse wrote in her notes that his appetite was decreased. The nurse phoned the third year family practice resident, Doctor Frazier, who came to the nursery to examine the patient."

I glanced over at Doctor Frazier, wearing a white coat and sitting in the second row with his thinning brown hair and frameless glasses. He had a blank, ashen look on his face. *God, I'd hate to be in his shoes,* I thought. *How hard this must be for him.*

Here Doctor Phillips uncomfortably paused. She took a deep breath and went on. "The nurse reported that Doctor Frazier thought the baby was fine, and he had no further recommendations. The nurse was concerned, though, and kept a close eye on the infant. Four hours later the baby began vomiting, and his rectal temperature was then 102 degrees.

"Doctor Frazier was once again summoned, and after his repeat examination, he phoned me and I immediately came to look at the patient. My examination revealed a lethargic white male in moderate distress. His pulse rate was two hundred, the rectal temperature was 103, his respiratory rate was 36, and his oxygen saturation was 95 %. His fontanelle was flat, his pupils were equal, round, and reactive to light. Ears and throat were normal, and his neck was supple. Cardiovascular exam revealed a tachycardia with a 2/6 holosystolic flow murmur, his lungs were clear, and the abdomen was soft, flat and non-tender, with normal liver and spleen. Capillary refill was normal."

"Clearly seriously ill," Doctor Garrison commented.

"Yes," she agreed. "At that point, a septic workup was performed, which included a CBC, blood cultures, a chemistry panel, urinalysis, chest x-ray, clotting studies, arterial blood gases and lumbar puncture. The child's white count was 23,000, markedly elevated, while his hemoglobin and hematocrit were normal. The prothrombin time was slightly elevated at 15, indicating the baby was septic, and the arterial blood gases demonstrated a metabolic acidosis with a pH of 7.3 and a bicarb of ten. The lumbar puncture, chest x-ray, urinalysis and other labs were unremarkable. IV Ampicillin and Gentamicin were promptly instituted. The baby was transferred to the neonatal intensive care unit, but his condition deteriorated. Four days later he went into cardiopulmonary arrest, and resuscitative efforts were unsuccessful. He died at 23:30."

Doctor Garrison shook his head and remarked, "How unfortunate. What did the autopsy show?"

Doctor Phillips said, "In short, the baby died from group B streptococcal sepsis."

"Thank you, Doctor Phillips," Doctor Garrison said as he slowly walked up, assisted by his cane, and took Doctor Phillips' place behind the lectern. The audience remained completely silent, shocked by what they had heard, and all present were glad they weren't the one who examined the baby that fateful day. Doctor Garrison stood there for a few moments, eyes looking downward, obviously gathering his thoughts.

Finally, he looked up at the crowd of doctors sitting in front of him and said, "Group B streptococcus, commonly abbreviated GBS, is the most common microorganism seen in sepsis, pneumonia and meningitis in the newborn. Around eight thousand babies in the United States contract GBS yearly, and around five percent of these babies die. Twenty to twenty-five percent of expectant mothers carry GBS in their rectum or vagina, and a baby can come in contact with this bacterium during childbirth. Someday, I hope that we will have a way to screen for GBS and treat it prophylactically, but that's not available now.

"So, our best hope to save infected babies is picking up the illness as early as possible, when the antibiotic regimen has the greatest opportunity to be effective. The initial signs and symptoms can be lethargy, irritability, poor appetite, hypothermia or elevated temperature, pale appearance or shortness of breath."

Doctor Garrison looked over at Doctor Frazier, who was leaning forward and had his face covered with his hands. "Doctor, in retrospect it seems clear that on your initial evaluation, Baby Edwards exhibited irritability, would you not agree?"

Doctor Frazier sighed and muttered, "Yes."

Doctor Garrison looked warmly at him. "Doctor Frazier, many of us sitting in this room would have likely missed this early presentation, but, remember GBS at the onset can have very subtle symptoms, and it is important to be aggressive if there is any suspicion whatsoever. Now, would the baby's life have been saved had the diagnosis and treatment been made four hours earlier? While it's impossible to say definitively, in my way of thinking, it seems unlikely."

Doctor Garrison added, "Doctor Frazier, do you have any further comments?"

Doctor Frazier stood and said, "Yes. One part of this case that has not been discussed is what happened during the cesarean section."

With his words, I felt like I'd been slapped in the face. *What?*

Doctor Frazier added, "I'd like to know if Doctor Conrad had any problems with the procedure he'd like to share with us."

A collective groan went up from my colleagues, and all turned to look at me. I felt blindsided and wanted to hide in a corner. I sat in stunned silence.

Abe observed my astonished state, and he stood and with a hint of anger in his voice, said, "I am the OB/GYN chief resident who attended the case. The cesarean went fine. There were no complications."

Doctor Garrison first glanced at me and then at Doctor

Frazier. With a knowing look, he said, "Very good. I hope we've all learned something from the case presented today. I know I certainly have. Thank you, Doctor Phillips, for your presentation."

"Any further questions or comments?" Doctor Garrison asked, looking back and forth at the audience for any raised hands.

Seeing none, Doctor Garrison said, "You are now dismissed."

As we emptied from the conference room into the hallway, Abe faced me and said, "Gary, you heard my words?"

I mutely nodded.

"Again, you know as well as I that the cesarean section went perfectly well. It seems to me that Doctor Frazier was looking to divert attention from him to someone else. In other words, he was looking for a scapegoat. I believe everyone, including Doctor Garrison, understood that. So keep your chin up, okay?"

"Will do. Thanks, Abe."

I somberly walked away, trying to put aside the shellshock of what had just happened. Doctor Frazier had delivered an unexpected insinuation, but I had to forget it for the time being. I still had a full day ahead of me, and other patients needed my attention. Later, I would have the chance to sit quietly, breathe and begin healing, but not now. Residents didn't have the privilege of taking a few days off to regroup when, for whatever reason, they were knocked off center.

In modern times, women are screened for GBS when they're between thirty-five and thirty-seven weeks pregnant. If their test is positive, they are given prophylactic antibiotics during labor, and the risk of the baby contracting the infection is extremely low. I'll likely never see another case like that one for the rest of my life.

As I look back on the situation, which happened almost thirty-nine years ago, I recognize that Doctor Frazier was simply trying to deflect some of the blame of this regrettable case onto me, his intended scapegoat.

Historically speaking, scapegoating is an ancient Jewish practice, performed once a year on Yom Kippur. On this sacred day, the high priest of Israel gathered two goats and placed them at the door of the tabernacle. One goat was sacrificed, while on the head of the second was symbolically laid the sins of the people. This goat—the scapegoat— was then driven out into the wilderness.

No longer a religious practice, contemporary scapegoating involves the selection of a group or an individual rather than a goat to carry one's errors, with the ultimate goal of self-cleansing. But the designated scapegoat can disarm the intentions with understanding and forgiveness.

So, thank you, Doctor Frazier, for teaching me a valuable lesson. Owning one's mistakes in life is not the easiest thing to do, but we all have to take accountability for our actions. Every spiritual practice demands it.

Now is the age of self-responsibility.

Not of scapegoating.

Chapter 25

BREAKING POINT

Every emergency physician experiences times jokingly known as "sphincter moments," situations when the events occurring are so intense and unnerving that the muscles of the rectum are purported to go into an uncontrollable spasm. While this often-talked-about concept is more metaphorical than reality-based, the paralyzing fears that "sphincter moments" represent are certainly part of the practice of emergency medicine.

These situations, often ones that defy easy solutions and invariably occur when a patient's life is on the line, demand that the physician and nursing staff act fast—or else. At these critical junctures, health care providers must grit their teeth and shoulder the burdensome responsibility that is their lot, knowing that they are as capable as any to deal with such crises. In the back of the physician's mind, though, a small part of him wishes that God, in His Infinite Wisdom, would intervene and find another worthy soul to step forward and manage these potentially disastrous cases.

But divine intercessions do not usually occur, and the ultimate onus rests on the doctor's own head. He, along with a dedicated nursing staff, must face the crises head on, "damn the torpedoes, full speed ahead," no matter how overwhelming and nerve-wracking the situations are that confront them.

In these gut-wrenching moments, the doctors and nurses know they have to keep their wits about them. While the family may be in a state of sheer panic, running about like chickens with their heads cut off, if the truth were known, the doctor and nurses usually feel just as frantic, yet they have to maintain a calm, competent façade. Health care providers are experts at hiding their feelings even during the most grim and intense moments, and they have to be, otherwise hysteria would rear its ugly head, and the entire emergency department would erupt into chaos and collapse like a cardboard house in a tornado.

Inevitably, after too many of these "sphincter moments," especially if the outcomes are not happy ones, the physician reaches a breaking point. This usually follows a number of upsetting events that have occurred in fairly quick succession, and rarely is just one episode enough to upset the physician's emotional and professional applecart. To those who are naïve to such happenings in emergency medicine, the following scenario is a not-too-atypical tale of how an emotional breakdown can be spawned.

Doctor Casey has just overseen the death of a young man from a drug overdose and spent some painful, tearful moments with his family. She is now introspectively sitting in front of the computer entering her notes on the case, when one of the nurses approaches.

"Doctor Casey?"

"Yes?"

"Another family member, I believe she's a sister of the overdose patient, has shown up and claims she has information that demonstrates the patient was actually murdered."

Doctor Casey raises her eyebrows. "Really?"

"Yes, when you have a chance, the family wants to talk with you again."

"Okay," replies Doctor Casey. She fidgets uncomfortably at her desk. She hasn't eaten in six hours, and she'd give anything to have a minute to go to the bathroom. She muses: *After I talk with the family, I'll call the Medical Examiner about the case, and then, maybe, the bathroom?*

She stands to go speak with the family, when Doctor Slimy, the hospitalist—a physician whose job is to admit and care for hospital patients—approaches and gives her the evil eye.

"Doctor," he argues as he scratches at his scraggly salt and pepper beard, sending small flecks of dandruff floating to the floor, "I don't understand why you admitted room six to me. I don't care if she's ninety and passed out, she doesn't need to be in the hospital."

Doctor Casey meets his stare with one of her own and shrugs her shoulders. "I disagree. Her EKG is abnormal, she has new-onset renal insufficiency, her hemoglobin is eight and her stool tests positive for blood. She needs to be in the hospital."

"Don't you know I've admitted seven patients in the past two hours?" Doctor Slimy complains. "I'm overwhelmed. If you feel that strongly about admitting her, first I want you to consult with the on call cardiologist, gastroenterologist and nephrologist." And just like that, at his whim, another thirty minutes of work have been foisted upon her.

"Doctor Slimy," she says, feeling inundated and a bit irritable, "I'm overwhelmed, too. You'll have to call them yourself."

As Doctor Slimy stomps away, he sneers and says, "To Hell with you."

Doctor Casey steels herself and fights off the urge to retort. At that moment, the nurse returns. "The family of the overdose wants to talk with you now. They say it's important."

"As soon as I can," Doctor Casey responds.

Then the emergency clerk approaches and lays a letter on

Doctor Casey's desk. "This just came for you."

"Why now?" Doctor Casey asks, seeing on her computer that the emergency examination rooms are all full, and twenty more patients are waiting in the front to be seen.

"From the letterhead, I'm guessing it's from a lawyer. I thought you wouldn't want to wait and find it in your mailbox tomorrow."

Doctor Casey wonders: *Is it a lawsuit? God, I hope not. I'll open it when things slow down. Now, about talking with that family . . .*

The clerk interrupts her thoughts. "Doctor Casey, just a moment ago, I received two phone calls for you. One is the Transfer Center, who informs me that Okmulgee Hospital wants to refer a head bleed in critical condition, and on the other line is a paramedic who needs to get orders for two patients he's bringing in Code 3—lights and sirens—from a high-speed motor vehicle accident."

"Okay, I'll get them both in a second."

An EMT walks up and asks, "Would you look at this EKG? This is a fifty-nine-year-old male with chest pain."

Doctor Casey initials it. "It's normal. Tell the nurse to start an IV and initiate a cardiac workup. I'll see him as soon as I can."

At that point, Greta, an emergency department physician associate, approaches and asks, "Doctor Casey, please look at this chest x-ray. I'm worried about the mediastinum. It looks a bit wide and could possibly be an aneurysm."

"Is the patient in any distress?" asks Doctor Casey.

"No, she looks fine."

"Good, then give me a moment to take these phone calls, okay?"

"Surely."

Persistent high-pitched wails erupt from a newly-checked in pediatric patient in the room next to Doctor Casey, while the sound of retching echoes from the adjacent room.

"Please help me," the vomiting patient cries as she sticks her head out of the room and throws up over a quart of bright-red blood into the hallway just before she passes out.

"I'll be right there," Doctor Casey answers.

To put it mildly, Doctor Casey is feeling more and more edgy. She tells the clerk, "I'm ready. Can you transfer those calls to me?"

"Yes, doctor, and when you're through with them, the hospital administrator wants to talk with you. It seems Doctor Slimy has filed a complaint."

"Damn it!" she yells at the top of her lungs. "I can't talk to her right now!" With that, she picks up the metal chart sitting on the desk in front of her and hurls it against the wall with a loud *clang*.

The hum of the emergency department suddenly stops and becomes as still as the inside of a hermetically-sealed casket buried underneath an Egyptian pyramid. Everyone mutely stares at Doctor Casey.

One of the nurses whispers to another, "I wonder why she's so upset?"

In an analysis in *Academic Emergency Medicine* in 2000, emergency department physicians from three different hospitals were followed by a researcher for 180-minute segments. In the study, tasks, interruptions and breaks-in-tasks were documented. An interruption was defined as an occurrence that briefly demanded the attention of the physician, but did not result in changing to a new duty. A break-in-task was considered to be an episode that demanded the attention of the doctor for more than ten seconds and resulted in changing to a new duty. The mean number of interruptions in the 180-minute study period was 30.9, while the mean number of breaks-in-task was 20.7. So, in these hospitals, the average number of interruptions and breaks-in-task happened once every three and a half minutes, leaving little time to sit and ponder complex cases.

Every physician has a different way of blowing a gasket. For me, my personal favorite, like Doctor Casey's, is grabbing a chart sitting on my desk and flinging it across the room, being certain that it doesn't hit anyone. I have also been known to spew out a string of profanities when the situation becomes too much to bear. I take care not to erupt in the midst of the chaos, but, rather, do so at some point in the future, so as not to detract from the care of my current patients. Just picture a stick of dynamite with a long, sparking, slowly burning fuse leading to it. Eventually it will explode—it's just a matter of time.

An example of emergency department madness occurred once to one of my colleagues, Doctor Robin. He was a Buddhist, and practiced his spirituality in a way that was apparent to everyone. He was centered, balanced, soft-spoken and never seemed to lose his temper. One fateful day, he was treating a critically ill patient with a myocardial infarction. He prepared the patient to go to the cardiac cath lab to have an angiogram, a procedure to detect arterial blockages, only to meet resistance from the cardiologist on call, who preferred instead to place the patient on anticoagulants and admit him to the intensive care unit.

Doctor Robin was certain his position was correct, but he felt boxed into a corner, without any recourse. So, without saying a word to anyone, he slowly walked into the break room, closed the door behind him and began flinging chairs against the wall. A short time later, he emerged, hoping his burst of anger might make him feel better, but it didn't.

I've always felt that the pressures of the emergency department have the potential to bring anyone to his or her knees. I suspect that if Jesus, Mary, Buddha, Mohammed or any saint or bodhisattva was miraculously transported into the role of an emergency physician, after trying to deal with the overpowering morass, they would all eventually be discovered in the break room, slinging chairs around with reckless abandon, and cursing like a sailor who lost his mother's home in a drunken game of poker.

I believe that many people subscribe to a spiritual misconception, in that the most enlightened beings are those who are always calm and collected, no matter the circumstances. The prototypical image for this ideal would be someone meditating in the lotus posture, repeating the *Om* mantra over and over, or perhaps a Benedictine monk sitting peaceably in the monastery, listening to his brothers as they performed Gregorian chants.

In contrast, I maintain that those who are most spiritual instead manifest a "full spectrum personality." In other words, these persons are completely capable of expressing themselves in all ways, even though the emotions may not be ones considered to be typically "spiritual." A biblical example of this occured when Jesus lost his cool in the temple, and he overturned the tables of the money changers and the benches of dove peddlers. If he had casually strolled in and calmly said, "Hey guys, I just talked with God and he wants you to leave the temple; you're being a bit too greedy and rowdy," the vendors would have laughed in his face and told him to get lost. I know there have been times in the emergency department when I have had to express controlled anger to motivate some of my patients and colleagues to do the right thing, yet I must confess that anger has also occasionally been directed at me when I was too hardheaded otherwise to budge from a wrong way of thinking.

So yes, even with doctors, who are supposed to be steady and controlled under all circumstances, the combination of "sphincter moments," associated with an overwhelming dose of chaos, can eventually lead to a breaking point, manifested by a crazed emotional outburst. This occasional, explosive behavior is all part of the equation, though, and as long as no one is harmed, and the instigator has a low threshold for apology, then acceptance, compassion and understanding must rule the day.

Over the years, I have discovered that, due to my episodic bad behavior, I have had to apologize more than occasionally to my fellow health care providers. Someday, perhaps, I'll get better control of my emotions, but, as I think about it, after forty years in the emergency department, that's highly unlikely. Like every one of us who walk the pathway of life, I'm only human.

Thank God the nursing staff in my emergency department understands that.

Chapter 26

AN UNWELCOME SURPRISE

The practice of emergency medicine is the granddaddy of continual, off-the-wall surprises. While struggling in the emergency trenches, oftentimes I wonder: *What will I be seeing next? Will the patient presenting be easy or challenging?*

Usually, the initial diagnosis is obvious in the first few moments of the physician's evaluation. On occasion, though, the caregiver can be caught completely off guard by the symptoms the patient first displays and the eventual diagnosis. I wish this sort of event were more rare than it is, but when the doctor has all the tools of modern medical technology to apply to a patient's care, unforeseen diagnoses completely unrelated to the original symptoms can be ascertained, ones which may not be pleasant discoveries.

I was sitting at my desk in the emergency department, looking at the computer, when I noticed with a sense of annoyance that five new patients had checked in. At that point, one of the nurses approached me, holding a notepad with some scribbles on it.

"Doctor Conrad," she asked, "I need to know if we can accept this patient."

"Okay," I respond. "Go ahead."

"The paramedic is on the scene of a seventy-four-year-old who fell nine feet off a ladder. He struck his head and was knocked unconscious for around thirty seconds. Now he is alert, and only complaining of pain in his left posterior chest where he hit the ground. The family is requesting that emergency medical services—EMS—bring him to our facility."

I quickly looked at the on-call list and replied, "Tell the paramedic that we have a general surgeon and neurosurgeon available. She can bring him here."

"Will do," she said.

A short time later, the patient arrived, and I walked into the room to evaluate him. Concerned family members sat at his bedside.

I glanced at his chart as I approached. His vital signs were stable.

"Mr. Webb," I said as I arrived at his bedside, "I'm Doctor Gary Conrad. I understand that you fell off a ladder?"

"Yes."

"Why did you fall?"

"I slipped off the rung while helping my son hang guttering."

"I see. You didn't pass out or feel dizzy to cause the fall?"

"No."

"I understand you hit your head."

"That's right."

"You were knocked unconscious?"

"Yes."

"Do you have a headache or vomiting?"

"No."

"Does your neck or back hurt?"

"No."

Immediately, by the brevity of his answers, I knew the patient was very stoical. Sometimes those who fall have a tremendous amount of anxiety and will animatedly spew out a number of complaints after such an incident, but I become most concerned about those who tolerate their symptoms, the ones who try hard to convince me that everything is okay. Over my years of seeing many patients of different ages, I have discovered that the older generations are much tougher than the more recent ones. As opposed to younger patients, they have experienced more hardships in life, and, overall, they seem better capable of handling the difficulties that confront them.

I ask, "Okay, how about your chest and abdomen?"

"My stomach is fine, but my ribs hurt behind my heart."

"Any regular medications?"

"Yes, just a pill for my prostate."

"Any blood thinners?"

"No."

"Do you smoke or drink?" It's my job to ask, even though I already knew the answer by looking at his skin, with the excessive number of wrinkles and sallow, unhealthy coloration.

"I've smoked a pack a day for forty years, but I don't drink."

"I see. May I take a look at you?"

He nodded.

My examination revealed an elderly, slender white male who was in mild distress. His pupils were equal, round and reactive to light, but he had a moderate amount of swelling on the back of his head. His heart and lungs sounded normal, though a severe amount of pain was exhibited as I palpated his left posterior ribs. His abdomen was soft, flat and non-tender, and his neurological examination was unremarkable.

I felt relieved that he seemed to have only a few areas of concern, but his stoicism, combined with his age and the height from which he fell, worried me.

Putting my stethoscope back around my neck, I said, "Sir,

we'll need to check an EKG, some blood and urine, as well as CAT scans to see how severe your injuries are. Would you like to have something for pain while we wait for the test results?"

I fully expected him to decline, but he answered, "Yes."

When I returned to my desk, I entered orders for his tests and pain medication on the computer.

Over the next few hours, Mr. Webb's workup gradually began to trickle in. Immediately, an EKG was performed, which was normal, and later his laboratory results returned, all of which revealed nothing unusual. The CAT scans invariably take longer, as the images are sent to a radiologist, who is often stationed at another location.

I first found the reports of his head and neck scans on the computer, and they were normal. A short time later, though, the clerk called over to me. "Doctor Conrad?"

"Yes?"

"I've got a call for you from the radiologist. He wants to give you a report."

When the radiologist calls, it's never good news, I thought. *Something must be awry.*

I picked up the phone. "Hello?"

"Hi, I'm Doctor Bunch. Is this Doctor Conrad?"

"Speaking."

"I'm calling about the CAT scan of the chest on Mr. Webb. Is he your patient?"

"He is."

"Well, he has some significant injuries from his fall. He has five broken ribs on the left side . . ."

I interrupted, "Which ones?"

"One through five," he answered.

His words concerned me. The higher the rib fractures the more severe the trauma. "He must have hit harder than I had guessed," I commented.

"Also, you need to know he also has a tiny lung collapse—a pneumothorax—on the left. My guess is that nothing will need to be done unless it enlarges."

"Good."

"But there's one more thing . . ."

I felt my heart in my throat. *What?*

"Does the patient have a history of lung cancer?"

"Not that I'm aware of."

"Well, brace yourself. The CAT scan of his chest also demonstrates lung cancer, likely a mesothelioma, in the left lung."

"Oh, no."

"I had guessed that wasn't expected, so I preferred to let you know by phone."

"Thank you," I said as I hung up. I paused for a moment to digest this devastating discovery. In no way was I prepared for this.

With a heavy heart, I walked into Mr. Webb's room. By this time, more of his worried family had gathered at his bedside.

"Hi, I'm Doctor Gary Conrad," I said to the newcomers. "Are you also family members?"

"Yes," they responded as a group.

I turned my attention to the patient. "Mr. Webb, I have some bad news to share with you. The injuries you sustained from the fall are moderately severe, but treatable. First, the good test results: The EKG and laboratories look okay, and even though you hit your head hard enough to render you unconscious, there are no blood clots in your brain."

I paused for a moment, feeling uncomfortable with the words I was about to say. "Now, the CAT scan of your chest shows five broken ribs, along with a small collapse of your left lung. The collapse is small enough that you likely will have no complications."

I took a deep breath and added, "But, the CAT scan also shows a tumor in your left lung, likely a type of cancer called a mesothelioma. Have you been exposed to asbestos in the past?"

Mr. Webb looked stunned. "I don't know."

"I know how hard this must be for you to hear. I'm sorry to have to tell you this news."

I glanced over at his family. They were understandably shocked, and tears welled in the eyes of some.

"Mr. Webb, I'll have to admit you to the intensive care unit, so we can watch for any difficulties that might occur because of your injuries. In the meantime, an oncologist will be asked to assess your cancer."

I raised my head and looked over at the family. "Anything else you'd like to know?"

After answering a few questions, I once again said, "I'm so sorry."

I turned and slowly walked out of the room.

I didn't look back—*I couldn't.*

Besides telling family members that their loved one has died, informing patients that they have cancer or some other potentially terminal disease is one of the hardest discussions to have in the emergency department. Yet, it's a task that I am required to perform more frequently than I would like.

While this dialogue is challenging for me to initiate, I know for the patient and family, hearing the "C word" has to be so much more difficult. In this particular case, the silver lining to the ominous, overhanging cloud was that by discovering the cancer earlier rather than later, the chance of successful treatment was somewhat increased. That said, unfortunately, mesothelioma, which is brought about by exposure to asbestos, is an aggressive type of cancer that has a poor prognosis, no matter when it is discovered.

When I walk out of the room after such discussions, I often reflect on what it would be like if a health care provider informed me that I had cancer, one that could possibly lead to my death. Telling someone of a dreaded diagnosis is certainly a difficult task, but how would I react personally to hearing this devastating news about myself? While such a question is nearly impossible to answer unless one is actually faced with such news, I'll give it my best shot, knowing such is, at best, speculation.

Assuming I don't drop dead while watching *It's a Wonderful Life* for the thirtieth time, and I have some time to prepare, I would hope to connect on some level with those that I love deeply, preferably face-to-face, when I could see the twinkle and caring in their eyes. Saying goodbye and sharing our innermost thoughts would be important for closure for everyone. In addition, I would attempt to see as many sunsets as possible. Like snowflakes, none are exactly the same, and to view God's handiwork in the glowing, effervescent sky would remind me of the preciousness and sacredness of every day of existence. Depending upon the severity of the pain I am experiencing, I would enjoy spending as much time in meditation as possible. I receive no greater joy than connecting with the Divine that exists within and without, and I believe that deepening my meditation practice would help prepare me for what Tibetan Buddhists call the bardo, the phases of existence that occur after death.

I have heard some say that as death approaches, they would contact those that they have harmed and express their regrets. While I think that's an admirable idea, I hope that before I draw near to the portals of death, I've already taken care of most of my apologies. I have no desire to burden my upcoming death with contrition and remorse. I have also heard some say that they would enjoy traveling to see the world. In my way of thinking, I would prefer the comforts of home, family and pets. To be away from my cozy abode in the time prior to The Great Transition would detract rather than add to my experience of death.

I believe Chief Tecumseh gave one of the best comments about death: "When it comes your time to die, be not like those whose hearts are filled with the fear of death, so that when their time comes they weep and pray for a little more time to live their lives over again in a different way. Sing your death song and die like a hero coming home."

We that practice in the emergency department deal with the diseases and deaths of others on a regular basis. We inform patients of difficult-to-hear diagnoses, and we tell families about the deaths of loved ones.

Preparing for our own deaths is an entirely different matter. As a younger man, I spent very little time thinking of dying, but as I age, I find myself pondering death more and more. Not in a dark, morbid way, but rather, realizing my life will someday end, I wish to enjoy each moment of living and breathing.

Now, the more I think about it, why wait until I am close to dying to see as many sunsets as I can?

Chapter 27

TIME MARCHES ON

A good night's sleep is an absolute necessity to be an effective emergency physician. Knowing this, when I work the early shift, I go to bed shortly after the sun does, setting my alarm for 5:20 a.m., understanding that I have to be up and at 'em by 5:25. Often I wake beforehand, and I lie in bed beside my sleeping wife and ponder the upcoming day. This early hour is a precious, sacred, and necessary time—a time when I steel myself in preparation.

The routine approximately follows this schedule: I wake and groggily glance over at the alarm clock, resting in its usual spot on the dresser across from our bed—4:50 a.m. I stand, stretch and walk across the room and flick off the man-made rooster. I return to the bed, gently ease myself down, and allow myself a few more minutes pondering and processing. Sometime later I check it again—5:05. I look over at Sheridan, curled up to my right, and find myself grateful that she has chosen to spend her life with me. I feel the warmth of her body through the sheets, yet I resist the urge to touch her, knowing she could wake and have a difficult time falling back asleep.

My mind shifts to other thoughts, and once again I peek at the clock—5:15. I become a bit restless; only ten more minutes can pass until I have to get up. I think about my profession as an emergency physician and wonder: *Why do I continue to throw myself into this maelstrom with all the stress it brings? What crisis, event, incident, quandary, jam, and yes, emergency, will I face today that will call on every bit of skill that I have for a successful resolution?*

And yet I know—without a doubt—that the breadth and depth of my experience in emergency medicine is valuable to patients who come to see me with their varied ailments. After almost forty years, my successes, and especially my failures, have helped me become a much better physician. On the tough days, this knowledge gives me solace.

Still, all those years is a long time to last as a physician in the world of emergency medicine, especially considering that we emergency physicians experience burnout at a rate of more than three times that of the average doctor. *Why have I been able to last this long?* It's a good question, and I'm not sure I have the answer.

The clock reads 5:23 a.m., and I find myself wishing I could stay in bed for longer than just two more minutes. Yet, time marches on, and there's nothing I can do to stop it.

I lie as still as a corpse, and the moment the clock changes to 5:25, I reluctantly pull the covers down and sit up on the edge of the bed, shoulders slumped ever so slightly. I sigh, take a few deep breaths, clasp my hands together and push my arms up over my head and stretch.

I rise from the bed.

The day begins, and I embrace it.

Whatever it may bring.

Chapter 28

THE ASTHMA ATTACK

Since I am viewed by my emergency medicine colleagues as a seasoned veteran, I am frequently asked if one case stands out in my mind after all the years of laboring in the trenches. As I reflect on my career, I must admit that much of the time I felt like the Little Dutch Boy with his finger in the dike, doing all I could to keep catastrophe at bay.

I am astonished at all I have experienced since July of 1978, when I started my practice, and some memories definitely rise above the others. I clearly recall the tragedy of the bombing of the Murrah Building in Oklahoma City on April 19, 1995, and how our emergency department received and treated a handful of the overflow patients, ones that the saturated hospitals in Oklahoma City were simply too overwhelmed to manage. Also memorable was the May 3, 1999, Bridge Creek–Moore tornado which had a measured wind speed of 301 MPH and devastated the city of Moore and parts of southern Oklahoma City, killing thirty-six people. Our emergency department was much like a war zone, and I'll never forget the horrific cases we treated.

I could go on, but even with all these tragedies considered, one particular case stands out in my mind, an event that occurred on September 25, 1994, when I was sixteen years into my emergency medicine practice, a date when I, along with a dedicated team of emergency nurses, EMTs and respiratory therapists, truly made a difference.

The shift volume in the emergency department that evening was brisk and busier than normal, but at 12:45 a.m. the flow had slowed to a trickle, and I was finally able to complete some long over-due chart work that I had to delay until I was not so swamped. In modern times, medical records are documented on a computer, but in that era of antiquity, all of our charting was still done on paper. While the computer is far superior in many ways, paper documenta-tion was much more efficient than spending time click-click-clicking on a computer. Not only did paper charting allow more time to be spent with patients, always a plus, in addition, more moments became available for me to snack, go to the bathroom, or simply let my mind take a needed break. If free time was especially plentiful, I would even take a peek at the crossword puzzle in the local newspaper.

Little did I know that in just a few seconds, the relative calm would explode into chaos, and I would have to deal with a life-or-death crisis, requiring every bit of skill that I possessed.

Linsey was an energetic, active twelve-year-old, a seventh grade honor student. She never let her seemingly-mild asthma in-terfere with her busy life, which included piano lessons, dance classes and show choir.

On that particular Sunday evening, she and her parents, Rick and Gloria, followed their usual routine, attending evening church services and meeting with friends for pizza afterward. After return-ing home, Linsey completed her homework and went to bed. Thirty minutes later, she suddenly woke and cried out to her mother, "Mom, I don't feel well. I can't breathe."

When Gloria heard her daughter's shout, she was sitting at the kitchen table watching *Star Trek* and grading school papers for her fourth grade class. She stood and headed for Linsey's bedroom, though when she arrived, she was horrified to find her daughter was having severe difficulty breathing, worse than she had ever seen.

Shaken, her mother told her, "Use your Ventolin inhaler," expecting the symptoms to be relieved momentarily. Linsey took two puffs without improvement, and Gloria grew more alarmed and yelled, "Rick, get out of bed. We've got to get Linsey to the hospital. She can't breathe."

Rick quickly threw on some clothes and met them in the hallway. They headed out the front door, and just before they reached the car, Linsey managed to say, "I don't think . . . I don't think I'm going to make it." She whispered to herself, "Please, God, don't let me die, and if I do, take care of me."

Fortunately, they lived only about a mile from the hospital, and they loaded into their car and sped through a dreary, foggy night. In the front seat across from her husband, Gloria kept a close watch on Linsey, who was restlessly sitting in the back. Just blocks away from the emergency department, her mother noticed an ashen appearance and a blank stare on her daughter's face. *Something is very, very wrong,* she thought. "We're . . . losing her, Rick," she frantically stammered out.

They arrived at the emergency entrance seconds later. Linsey's mother jumped out of the car and ran inside to get help, while her father opened the back door to get his daughter. To his dismay, he discovered her slumped over unconscious. When he turned Linsey toward him to lift her out of the car, he saw that her lips were turning blue.

"My daughter can't breathe," I heard a frantic voice yell. I

threw down the chart I was working on, stood and hurriedly headed toward the shout. I, along with a group of nurses, converged on a man holding a lifeless, unresponsive child. I guessed her age to be in the early teens. Following close behind was a woman who I figured was her mother.

I yelled to one of the nurses, "Call respiratory therapy, *STAT!*"

Another nurse took her from her father's arms and carried her to a stretcher in a room. "Please wait in the hallway," I tersely asked the parents as I followed my young patient into the room.

I rushed to the side of the stretcher and saw an adolescent who was cyanotic—blue—and in severe respiratory distress, with an oxygen saturation in the 80s, far too low to maintain her young life. Normally, in asthmatics, wheezing is the hallmark symptom, but her difficulty in breathing was so severe there were no breath sounds at all. I had to act quickly, for if this continued, at the minimum she could experience brain damage, or at the worst, she could die. I knew I needed to intubate her—put a breathing tube in her airway—immediately. A nurse had already started to assist her ventilations with an Ambu bag, a hand-held device commonly used to provide needed oxygen to patients having respiratory distress.

I said to the nurses, "Start an IV and call for lab and x-ray *now*."

At that moment, a respiratory therapist wearing navy scrubs burst into the room. I directed her, "Set the patient up for intubation."

She pulled out the airway tray and opened it up on a stand at the bedside. She asked, "What size endotracheal tube would you like?"

For a child, the best way to determine the correct diameter of the tube was to pick one that closely matched the size of the little finger. "Get me a four and a five," I requested. The respiratory therapist placed both of them before me as I positioned myself at the head of the bed. I placed the tubes next to the patient's hand. The five was perfect.

"Give me a small curved intubation blade and please set up suction," I added. The intubation blade is a tool that holds the airway open and allows the practitioner to see the epiglottis, and eventually, the trachea. I pumped up the bed to raise the patient to a position satisfactory to insert an airway into her throat.

The bed now in the proper location, I checked the light on the blade and put air in and out of the intubation tube cuff to be certain it was intact. *We're ready to go,* I thought, *but there's no time to spare.* Her lethargy and blue discoloration were increasing moment to moment.

Putting my hand under her chin and pointing it upward, I placed the intubation blade in the back of her throat, pushing her tongue to the side in hope of visualizing the epiglottis, the structure that prevents food and fluids from getting into the airway when swallowing. Mentally, I rehearsed the steps to take. Once seen, I would put pressure at its base with the tip of the blade, which would move the epiglottis forward, out of the way so I could have sight of her trachea and vocal cords. At that point I would place the breathing tube—an endotracheal tube—into her windpipe.

But I didn't get that far. My young patient, in her altered state of consciousness, began to struggle and fight. Even though she was nearly comatose, she was still able to sense that I was putting something into her throat, her gag reflex was activated, and she began to vomit.

At that point, I placed a suction catheter in the back of her throat and removed copious amounts of vomit, which was obstructing my view of her airway. I steeled myself and tried again. Once again, she gagged and vomited. Again, I suctioned her throat clear.

I took a deep breath. She needed an airway now. "Hand me the smaller tube, the four," I directed the respiratory therapist.

I asked a nearby nurse, "Hold her head still and pull her chin up."

Tube in hand and her head immobilized, I advanced the tube into the right nostril. The placement of a nasotracheal tube—what I was attempting—largely bypasses the gag reflex, so in a semiconscious patient, the physician might have better success. This is usually not tried initially because the attempt can cause difficult-to-control bleeding from the nose, and it is blind—one cannot see the vocal cords. I patiently advanced the tube, hoping and praying that it would find its mark—the trachea.

Much to my relief, after a brief episode of choking, the tube moved into her airway. I listened for breath sounds; they were equal bilaterally, and now that air was being forced into her lungs, I heard wheezing.

Thank God . . .

"Fix the tube in position and put her on a ventilator," I directed the respiratory therapist. "Next give her 5 milligrams of Albuterol and 0.5 milligrams of Atrovent by nebulizer, followed by continuous Albuterol nebulizer treatments."

Seeing the IV was in place, I told a nurse, "Please give her a liter of normal saline and 10 milligrams of Decadron IV. Also, I want her to have 0.3 mg of epinephrine subcutaneously. I need a STAT portable chest x-ray for tube placement."

Over the next ten to fifteen minutes, I watched as her oxygen saturations gradually increased into the mid 90s. As her oxygenation improved, neurologically she remained intact, moving her arms and legs, and her pupils were equal, round and reactive. Now that the crisis had passed, a chart was handed to me, and I at-long-last discovered my young patient's name—Linsey.

While it was too early to tell for certain, every indication pointed to the likelihood that she would be fine. I would chat with the family in a few moments to let them know that their daughter had turned the corner, but for one moment, I closed my eyes in relief and, once again, thanked God.

As I hoped, Linsey did well in the hospital. She was admitted to the ICU and woke up the next morning with tubes in both nostrils, one that I had placed to support her breathing, and another that had been passed by the nursing staff from her nose into her stomach to keep her stomach empty, preventing aspiration of the stomach contents into her lungs.

Linsey's only memories of her emergency experience consisted of distant voices and vague, floating images. She retained no recollection of me, the nursing staff, or the respiratory therapist who teamed together to save her life. Four days after she was admitted, she was discharged home, free once again to live the busy, energetic life of an adolescent.

Time passed, and as I started writing this book, I began to wonder what had become of Linsey. Emergency physicians rarely know the eventual outcomes of their patients, and to obtain follow-up is rare indeed, unless, of course, a bad result occurs and a lawyer comes knocking. Fortunately, one of the nurses who had worked in the emergency department knew Linsey and her family through her church, and a meeting was arranged with Linsey and her father at a local restaurant. Regrettably, her mother had a previous commitment and was unable to attend.

I arrived a bit early, curious beyond words about what I would discover. I didn't wait long before Linsey and her father, Rick, walked through the door. I was taken aback by the change in their appearances, but after all, hadn't twenty-two years passed since I had seen them? While, generally, I don't recall how patients or their families look, when an experience occurs that is highly charged, memories have a tendency to be sharper, more well-defined, and small, insignificant details tend to stick in one's mind.

The two of them looked like a father-daughter match, as she was tall, slender, around 5' 8", with blue eyes and long dark hair, wearing black slacks and a black and white top. Rick appeared much younger than his age, and he was a bit taller than Linsey, with trimmed, graying hair and blue eyes. He wore glasses and a long-sleeved red shirt and dark gray slacks. Counting the years since 1994, I knew that Linsey was now thirty-four years old.

After we ordered food and took our places at a table, I asked Linsey, "Please tell me what has happened since I treated you all those years ago."

"Well," she said, "the good news is that I never again had an asthma attack as severe as that one so long ago. My pulmonologist thought that that episode was likely brought on by an allergic reaction to some ingredient in the pizza I ate that night."

"I see."

"Much later, I graduated as one of the valedictorians in high school, and after four years of college, received a B.A. in Journalism. I was married, later divorced, though I have recently remarried and now have three children. Adeline, my oldest daughter, is nine years old, my second daughter is Blakely, eight, and my boy, Ricky, is fourteen months old."

"You must be proud of them."

"Yes, I am extremely proud of my children; they are the lights of my life. They wear me out with all of their activity, but I am so thankful for them. I am even grateful for my first marriage and the stress of the divorce, because without marrying my daughters' father, I would have never had them. My son, from my second marriage, represents another chance for me. I've had a life of second chances—like that time in your emergency room—and I am thankful for those."

I asked, "What do you do for a living?"

"When I was fresh out of college, I was a marketing and public relations specialist for a surgical center for two years. For the next four years, I was a stay-at-home mother."

"That is one of the hardest jobs of all."

"Yes," she agreed. "After that, I was a high school English and Journalism instructor for five years. Currently, I am a legal assistant."

"Did you enjoy teaching?"

"Very much."

"Why did you leave?"

"Teaching was never in my long-term plan, but it's what worked for us, at least for a while. As a single mother, I needed a job I could work alongside my girls' schedule, and with snow days and school breaks. I struggle to do anything halfway, though, and teaching high school, with its sometimes-overwhelming responsibilities, took over my life. Now, since I am no longer teaching, I'm a better mother to my children when I'm not trying to meet the needs of others."

"In other words," I said, "like any good mother, you decided to make your own children a priority."

"Exactly. Besides," she added, "I'm sure you already know, public education is under attack, and that sad fact is especially true in Oklahoma. The hostile environment our state legislature has created with the spending cuts in education inadvertently provided the push I needed to finally leave the classroom."

I chimed in, "I'm proud to say that my mother was a schoolteacher, and my sister followed in her footsteps. Like you, though, I'm appalled and embarrassed by the lack of our state's commitment to education."

I sighed and looked over at Rick, "Tell me about you."

Rick smiled and said, "I was a grade school principal for thirty years, though now I am retired from that position, and I am currently serving on the city council and sell insurance."

"Very good. Rick, I'd like to hear your thoughts about Linsey and the events that took place all those years ago."

"Certainly," he replied. "When I look back to the night that Linsey had the asthma attack and almost died, I can't help but think how different our lives could have been. Linsey has an amazing voice, and we would have never been able to hear her sing at talent shows, church, school, and beauty pageants, and more recently, at her grandfather's funeral. He died last year, and he had told her repeatedly that he wanted her to sing at his funeral."

"How wonderful that must have been," I said.

"It was," Rick confirmed. "As I think about it, if Linsey had not lived, we would have missed the special days such as high school and college graduation, and there would have never been a wedding for her and her mother to plan. We would have missed the early morning call telling us 'We're on our way to the hospital' for the births of our three grandchildren. Each call to go to the hospital has been special to her mother and me."

I nodded. "I can only imagine."

"You see, Doctor Conrad, Linsey is our only child. If she had died, there would be no grandchildren in our lives. More precious than gold is hearing 'Mamaw or Papaw' coming from small voices who love us."

Tears came into his eyes as he said, "I can't imagine what life would be like without them. We would not be looking forward to another family vacation at the beach. No sandcastles would be built, no running and playing on the beach."

"It would be a different world, wouldn't it?" I affirmed.

"Yes," he replied. "Traumatic events affect people for the rest of their lives. Fortunately for us the outcome was positive. We felt so blessed by how the events turned out. I know that we were literally seconds away from a different outcome, a different life. We will forever be grateful and thankful to you and the emergency staff at the hospital."

I found myself humbled by his words. "You are so welcome," I quietly said.

I glanced over at Linsey. "What are your thoughts?"

After hearing her father's words, Linsey paused and took a deep breath before she spoke. "Nothing in my adult life has been a straight path, and I've learned, for the most part, to embrace the chaos. But since that night so many years ago, I have carried in my mind the reminder that comes from the providence and grace that God granted me. I live with the responsibility to make this chance at life count, no matter how many times I've wondered why God didn't just go ahead and take me while He had me so close.

"I grew up believing that if I followed the rules of my church and my parents' household and went to college—if I met requirements and checked off all the lists—that life would fall into place. I would have everything I needed, my children would be perfect little angels who made straight As in school and excelled at everything they attempted. And, of course, my marriage would be blissful."

Linsey had a distant look in her eyes as she added, "As you might guess, that hasn't been the case. One of my daughters was diagnosed with speech apraxia, and she didn't speak until after she turned three. Then I suffered a miscarriage, the first in my extended family, and later I went through a divorce, after believing that would *never* happen in my life. I have come to realize that so much of what we experience in this world is completely beyond our control. Mindfulness matters more than anything, and being present in the moment is far more important than plans we make or checklists we complete. My path has been a twisted journey when compared to many, but that's okay. Once, back in 1994, there was a medical team whose mindfulness, in those crucial seconds, saved me. I was able to go forward, however imperfectly, and I was given a chance to live in this world."

I find myself blessed by her words. I had nothing to say.

She continued, "Luke 12:48 says, 'Everyone to whom much was given, of him much will be required, and from him to whom they entrusted much, they will demand the more.' So, no matter how stressed or anxious I may become, it all comes down to this. The chance I was given lent itself to a lifetime of responsibility. Sometimes, I wish I didn't have to carry that burden, but I am forever grateful to have learned what it means to live.

"Think about it. I would have never had a positive pregnancy test, and felt my water break and known I had a baby on the way.

I would have never watched my daughters dance on stage or play soccer or hear their sweet voices asking for donuts in the morning. I would have never picked up the phone, after going through a divorce, and told a man I met when I was eighteen years old that he was my love, and I had never let him know.

"Oh, and by the way," she said with a twinkle in her eyes, "he's now my husband."

"What a wonderful story," I commented.

"Isn't it?" she added with a smile.

Becoming more serious, she went on, "I also have fear, though, that comes from the power I know my asthma has over me. I watched my baby girl struggle through RSV—respiratory syncytial virus—that almost took her from me. I have three asthmatic children, and I despise the disease. I rush to my daughters' bedside when I hear them coughing during the night. I sleep with my one-year-old son inches from me, and the nebulizer machine sits by my bed for easy access."

"Given your baptism by fire," I said, "your reactions seem perfectly normal to me."

"I suppose you're right. Yet, the fact is that I have been so blessed. It's tough to put into words adequately what my experience at your hospital has meant to me and my parents. I now have a beautiful family, and whatever problems I've faced in my life, the bottom line is that I'm alive, and that's what matters."

"Linsey," I said, starting to feel emotional. "Of course, you're right. I'm so glad you lived, and," I added, glancing at her father, "I'm happy you have a daughter and grandchildren to enjoy."

Shortly afterward, once we had finished our meal, we said our farewells. Somehow, at that precious, sacred moment, all of the inherent issues and problems of being an emergency physician—the challenging patients, the difficult shifts, the deaths, the regrets, the conflicts, the misjudgments, and even the lawsuits—quietly faded into the background, dwarfed by the results of this one weighted occasion back in 1994.

Warmth filled my heart, and as I pondered that time, when the normally stable universe teetered around a critical focal point, one that could have resulted in an unwanted, alternate reality, I felt grateful that I was able to be a steadier of the precariousness. A young life was saved, and I was part of the effort.

And there's nothing better than that.

Nothing.

EPILOGUE

Lord, make me an instrument of your peace: where there is hatred, let me sow love; where there is injury, pardon; where there is doubt, faith; where there is despair, hope; where there is darkness, light; where there is sadness, joy.

O divine Master, grant that I may not so much seek to be consoled as to console, to be understood as to understand, to be loved as to love. For it is in giving that we receive, it is in pardoning that we are pardoned, and it is in dying that we are born to eternal life.

—Saint Francis of Assisi

Heavenly Father, help me in this day to be a good and loving servant, and may I do the best job that I can to help others in my work in the emergency department. Bless me, guide me, be with me in all things that I do, and in all decisions I make.

—My morning prayer

Nothing goes on forever, and as George Harrison once sang, "All Things Must Pass." Now, after forty years in emergency medicine, I somberly realize that the end of my career is approaching.

Why, one might ask? Certainly, one reason is the speed at which I see patients has dropped dramatically. Quality is more important than quantity. The older I get, the more I have a tendency to be extra methodical and careful, and want to be thorough when I listen to the patients' stories, so that I might better understand the reasons they came to see me. What little clues might I miss if I don't listen with full attention? What is the undercurrent to the history—that which is not necessarily spoken? Perhaps the looks on their faces, the subtle mannerisms and signs, ones that will help me solve the conundrum of their health issues? I am no longer the hare, rather, the tortoise. At this stage in my career, rapid patient turnover is no longer important to me except when the emergency department is completely inundated, and, in that case, emergency physicians just have to take their chances and do the best they can. The possibility a mistake will be made, though, is amplified greatly the faster health care practitioners work.

For a period of time, I had a short-lived practice in Integrative Medicine, based at my home. According to the University of Arizona, where I completed a fellowship in Integrative Medicine in 2008, this practice is defined as "healing-oriented medicine that takes account of the whole person, including all aspects of lifestyle. It emphasizes the therapeutic relationship between practitioner and patient, is informed by evidence, and makes use of all appropriate therapies."

Unfortunately, the raising of three daughters and my full-time employment in emergency medicine simply didn't allow the time necessary to continue this practice. While I was at it, though, I spent a minimum of an hour with each patient, and as I ponder that endeavor, one particular case stands out in my mind. After that patient had made several visits, I discovered to my dismay that my recommendations had not benefitted him whatsoever. He later said, though, that by the simple act of listening and fully hearing his story, he felt no small measure of comfort and was greatly pleased, no matter the indifferent outcome. In the current era, with the time constraints placed on physicians, rarely is the patient's complete history heard. While I never will be able to spend as much time with my emergency patients as I did in my home practice, I do the best I can to understand what they're trying to say.

While I believe my diagnostic skills are better than ever, another pressing issue is that I can't multi-task as well as I have in the past. The ability to focus on many things at one time is an absolute necessity to be an effective emergency physician. For me, to be certain that I keep close track of all of my patients, I have to methodically and repeatedly reassess their situations, their lab tests, x-rays, EKGs and such, to be certain I'm not overlooking something important, something critical. The "primrose path" in medicine occurs when a diagnosis appears too easy, too straightforward, and masks a much more serious condition, fooling all but the most analytical practitioner. To sort out the *milieu* of a patient's illness takes time, and while I've had plenty of practice at doing so, the uncomfortable truth is that I'm not as quick at making a diagnosis as I once was.

Besides, I must confess that certain unsavory aspects of emergency medicine have gradually taken their toll on me. One problem that has worsened over the years is dealing with drug seekers, those who come to emergency departments to obtain controlled substances, either to sell on the street for profit or to use personally in an abusive, addictive manner. While I want to be supportive of anyone who has pain, to sort out those whose suffering is real from those who are faking their ailments can be extremely challenging. In the face of this daily onslaught, the emergency physician's life force and compassionate nature are gradually siphoned away. Most of us have become exhausted by arguing with con artists who demand narcotics for their chronic pain, especially when their records clearly show that they received a plentiful supply in the recent past.

Another issue that continues to be a problem in emergency medicine is the medico-legal climate. For those who have been sued, as I have been, fear of litigation is a real issue and a driver for all sorts of unnecessary testing. No right-minded physician wants to go to court and be picked apart by a pompous attorney who doesn't care about the right or wrong of things, instead preferring to win and make big dollars for himself and his client, no matter the emotional, mental, and spiritual cost to the physicians who did the best they could. How many times have I ordered laboratory and x-ray studies simply to protect myself from the nightmare of the courtroom? Far more than I would like to admit.

Another dilemma frustrating to the emergency physician is the great disparity in the availability of health care for people from different socioeconomic strata. For true emergency situations, everyone is treated the same and is afforded high quality care, whether the patient is the CEO of a giant corporation or someone who lives in a cardboard box under the interstate highway. The problem arises when the situation is viewed to be non-critical. For example, if the president of the local bank appears at the hospital with biliary colic, an extremely painful condition where stones form in the gallbladder and obstruct the flow of bile, the gallbladder will be removed by the surgeon on call, and the issue will never happen again. Conversely, if someone from the poor side of town—in other words, a person with no insurance—shows up in the emergency department with the same problem, her acute pain would certainly be treated, and she might be admitted for observation, but her diseased gallbladder would stay inside her abdomen because its removal is not considered an emergency medical condition. I might guess, though, that one who visits an emergency department every few weeks to control her recurrent pain and vomiting from an unhealthy gallbladder might have a different opinion.

Another pitiful example of inequity in medical care occurs with insulin-dependent diabetics. If such patients have insurance, they're golden, and the gilded, majestic power of our health care system opens up before them. Their primary care provider will make sure they have a way to monitor their blood sugars at home and perhaps will provide them an insulin pump for better control. Dietary suggestions are made, and everything possible is done to keep their client out of diabetic ketoacidosis (DKA), a potentially life-threatening condition. On the other hand, the uninsured are lucky if they can find a free clinic that will help them with their basic diabetic supplies. If not, these patients must regularly visit emergency departments to get refills of the insulin and syringes. Unfortunately, their blood sugar levels are not tracked, and they present much more often with DKA, the risk of death increasing with every episode. Regretfully, these are just a few examples of a health care system that provides different tiers of care, depending on whether the patient is a have or a have-not.

Inappropriate end of life management is another predicament that drives emergency physicians absolutely insane. As a group, we do everything we can to help someone who has the sudden onset of a precipitous life-threatening condition. But what if the patient is ninety-two years old, has severe dementia, is given nutrition through a feeding tube placed in the upper part of the abdomen and has a catheter in the bladder to drain the urine? What if he also has infected pressure sores on the back and hips because of lying immobile in the bed for days on end? By any stretch of the imagination, recovery from such a combination of baseline conditions is simply not possible. The difficulty arises when the patient's family informs the caregiver that they want every action taken to extend life, including artificial life support. What is the healthcare practitioner to do? While the physician has the right to withhold extreme measures to those who, in their estimation, have no chance to recover, he or she does so at great risk for litigation. In general, our Western society has an overwhelming, unreasonable fear of the natural process called death, and to place the physician in the middle of such an ethical dilemma is patently unfair.

So, now that I'm in the twilight of my career, I find myself wondering what will be my legacy in emergency medicine. How will I be remembered? While I believe this is an understandable question from anyone who steadily and unavoidably walks toward the end of his occupation, the reality is that there can be no everlasting legacy. All of the streets named for famous people, the statues and museums erected in their honor, with the ravages and inexorable progression of time, will all be forgotten someday—no exceptions. For me in particular, one hundred years from now, no one will recall that I ever walked on this Earth. My *persona*, Gary D. Conrad, will not be recalled in any way, unless someone runs across a tattered copy of one of my books on a dusty shelf of an antique store.

Until that distant time comes, while I might be remembered for some heroic deed that saved someone's life, I believe I will mostly be recalled for little things, small acts of love that made a difference.

Perhaps some of my patients will recall when I assured them that I would give them relief from their pain—and I did. Maybe a frightened little girl, one scared out of her mind, will remember when I cajoled her and asked what her boyfriend's name was, making her feel a bit more comfortable and bringing a smile to her face. Possibly a family will recall, when they were faced with the impending death of a loved one, how they found comfort in my expressed belief that death is not an end, only a transition. And the list goes on and on.

I am grateful for all of the patients I have been allowed to serve. Working in the emergency department has pressed me up to and sometimes beyond the limits of my abilities, and much like an initiatory rite, helped me grow into a better person. In truth, I can't think of a more befitting profession where my capabilities could have been more suitably utilized, and where I could have served humankind better.

I think of emergency physicians when I hear the words of Erma Bombeck, "When I stand before God at the end of my life, I would hope that I would not have a single bit of talent left, and could say, 'I used everything you gave me.'"

What comes next, you might ask? I am reminded of when, on April 19, 1951, General Douglas MacArthur gave a farewell address before both houses of Congress. Eight days previously, he had been fired by President Harry S. Truman from his position as top commander of the American forces in the Korean War. He said in that speech:

". . . I still remember the refrain of one of the most popular barrack ballads of that day which proclaimed most proudly that 'old soldiers never die, they just fade away.' And like the old soldier of that ballad, I now close my military career and just fade away, an old soldier who tried to do his duty as God gave him the light to see that duty. Good-bye."

I believe that retiring emergency physicians have much in common with those old soldiers. Fatigued from the intense battleground of emergency medicine, they need rest and healing from all of their years of struggles in "The Pit," and at some point, they just fade away.

When I hang up my stethoscope and walk out of the doors of the emergency department for the final time, I will have no regrets, and I certainly have no plans to become sedentary. I will continue to write books, and, Good Lord Willing, there are many more waiting to spring forth when my mind is unfettered from the challenges of the emergency department. Writing has become the balm that keeps my mind and spirit healthy.

Much like emergency medicine once was.

ACKNOWLEDGMENTS

My odyssey through the chapters of *The Pit* could not have been accomplished without a number of helpers. First, I thank my primary editor and friend, Dr. Gladys Lewis. As a retired registered nurse and PhD English professor, she is uniquely qualified to add her suggestions, not only concerning the medical aspects, but also the developmental, grammatical, and stylistic structure of the book. She previously assisted me in the editing of my fourth book, *Murder at Stonehenge: A Daniel "Hawk" Fishinghawk Mystery,* and working with her has become as comfortable and peaceful as sailing on a calm, reflective sea into a familiar harbor.

Next, I express my deepest appreciation to my pal, Dr. Chris Corbett. As some of you may recall, Chris is a superb photographer and took the author photos for my first three books. At a later time, though, I discovered that he possessed excellent editorial skills. We agreed, for the modest fee of a sushi meal for every chapter reviewed, that he would contribute his services for the book, a proverbial win-win situation.

Also, many thanks to my friend, Marilyn Ratzlaff, who was of major assistance in performing the nitty-gritty, nuts and bolts labor required for the construction of *The Pit*. Not only that, she provided yet another editorial voice, and this book is far better due to her masterful contributions.

While he had nothing to do with the preparation of the book, I wish to make known my gratitude to Dr. Andrew Weil, to whom this book is dedicated. I met Andy in the summer of 1994 at a nutritional medicine seminar at the Feathered Pipe Ranch, situated near Helena, Montana. I had interest at the time in what was then termed alternative medicine, and meeting him eventually led me to complete the integrative medicine fellowship at the University of Arizona. Since then, my practice in emergency medicine has been pleasantly tinged with Andy's influence, and more than occasionally I will offer out-of-the-box integrative suggestions to my patients, ones that are unlikely to be found in any conventional medical texts.

I am also thankful to those who advised me on this book: Dr. Cameron Halsell, Patricia Rogers, Dr. Don Wilbur, Dr. Kinde Aguilar, Alex Scott and Dr. Cliff Wlodaver.

I owe the greatest debt of gratitude to the many nurses, physician associates, nurse practitioners, paramedics, EMTs, respiratory therapists, x-ray personnel, ultrasound technicians, and clerks with whom I have worked through the years. High quality patient care in the emergency department requires a team approach, and when an outcome is good, at times too much credit is attributed to the physician. I couldn't have done my life's work without these highly trained providers laboring at my side, and I will always be deeply appreciative of their expertise and assistance.

ABOUT THE AUTHOR

Gary D. Conrad lives with his wife, Sheridan, and their dogs, Karma and Buddy, in Edmond, Oklahoma. Gary is an emergency and integrative physician, and his interests include Tibetan rights, meditation, the music of Joseph Haydn, choral work and wilderness hiking.

He received his undergraduate diploma from Oklahoma State University, his M.D. degree from the University of Oklahoma, and after finishing his internship in 1978, has been a practitioner of emergency medicine in the greater Oklahoma City area. He has also completed a fellowship in integrative medicine at the University of Arizona.

Gary is the award-winning author of *The Lhasa Trilogy*, *Oklahoma Is Where I Live* and *Other Things on My Mind*, *Murder on Easter Island: A Daniel 'Hawk' Fishinghawk Mystery* and *Murder at Stonehenge: A Daniel 'Hawk' Fishinghawk Mystery*. He is currently working on a sequel to *The Lhasa Trilogy*.

He can be reached at his website, GaryDConrad.com.

Made in the USA
Columbia, SC
09 August 2019